D1605744

EDUCATION AND REVOLUTION IN NICARAGUA

The Praeger Special Studies
Series in Comparative Education

General Editor: **Philip G. Altbach**

Published in Cooperation with the
Comparative Education Center,
State University of New York, Buffalo

(continued on last page)

EDUCATION AND REVOLUTION IN NICARAGUA

ROBERT F. ARNOVE

PRAEGER

New York
Westport, Connecticut
London

Library of Congress Cataloging-in-Publication Data

Arnove, Robert F.

Education and revolution in Nicaragua.

Bibliography: p.
Includes index.
1. Education – Nicaragua. 2. Education and state –
Nicaragua. 3. Education – Social aspects – Nicaragua.
4. Literacy – Nicaragua. I. Title.
LA461.A75   1986   370'.97285   86-8187
ISBN 0-275-92138-7 (alk. paper)

Library of Congress Catalog Card Number: 86-8187
ISBN: 0-275-92138-7

First published in 1986

Praeger Publishers, 521 Fifth Avenue, New York, NY 10175
A division of Greenwood Press, Inc.

Printed in the United States of America

∞™

The paper used in this book complies with the Permanent
Paper Standard issued by the National Information Standards
Organization (Z39.48-1984).

10 9 8 7 6 5 4 3 2 1

Contents

v

Acknowledgments

Research for this book was supported by the Office of Graduate Research and Development and the President's Council on International Programs of Indiana University. Minister of Education Carlos Tünnermann Bernheim provided his good offices for arranging interviews with various Ministry of Education officials and policy makers in other governmental agencies. Leyla Saborío de Martínez and Adelayda Centeno Osorio graciously assisted me in making arrangements for interviews. The staff of the Office of Rural Nuclearization (NER) and the Project for the Elaboration and Reproduction of Educational Materials (PERME) were particularly helpful in providing transportation to various parts of the country and in accompanying me on field visits. Juan Bautista Arrien, Vice-Minister of Education for Planning, Rebecca de los Ríos of the Ministry of Planning (MIPLAN), and Mariano Vargas Narváez of the National University Council (CNES) met with me on multiple occasions and provided valuable criticism of my observations and impressions. Frank Barquero of the Ministry of Education was an invaluable research assistant, guide, and companion. To all those administrators, educators, and students, who were willing to take time from their busy schedules to meet with me and share their insights and information, I express my appreciation and my hope that I have been able to convey a realistic and accurate portrayal of the Nicaraguan education system during a critical period in its reformulation and transformation.

Nicaragua

Map from Thomas W. Walker, *Nicaragua: The Land of Sandino* (1981)
By permission of Westview Press

List of Acronyms

AA   Student Assistants
               Alumnos Ayudantes
AMNLAE   Nicaraguan Women's Association "Luisa Amanda Espinoza"
               Asociación de Mujeres Nicaragüenses "Luisa Amanda Espinoza"
ANDEN   National Association of Nicaraguan Educators
               Asociación Nacional de Educadores de Nicaragua
ANS   Asociación de Niños Sandinistas
               Sandinista Children's Association
AP   People's Literacy Teachers
               Alfabetizadores Populares
ATC   Rural Workers' Association
               Asociación de Trabajadores del Campo
CADIN   Chamber of Nicaraguan Industries
               La Cámara de Industrias de Nicaragua
CCC   Confederation of Chambers of Commerce
               La Confederación de Cámaras de Comercio
CDS   Sandinista Defense Committees
               Comites de Defensa Sandinista
CEP   Popular Education Collective
               Colectivo de Educación Popular
CEPA   Agrarian Education and Promotion Center
               Centro de Educación y Promoción
CEPAD   Evangelical Committee to Promote Development
               Comité Evangelico Pro Ayuda al Desarrollo
CIA   U.S. Central Intelligence Agency
CIDCA   Center for Investigation and Documentation of the
                    Atlantic Coast
               Centro de Investigación y Documentación de la Costa Atlantica
CISAS   Center for Information and Consulting Services in Health
               Centro de Información y Servicios de Asesoría en Salud
CNA   The National Literacy Crusade
               Cruzada Nacional de Alfabetización
CNES   National University Council
               Consejo Nacional de la Educación Superior
CPC   Popular Cultural Center
               Centro de Cultura Popular
CST   Sandinista Workers' Central
               Central Sandinista de Trabajadores
CUS   Council of Trade Union Unification
               Consejo de Unificación Sindical
EAC   Peasant Agricultural School
               Escuela Agropecuaria Campesina
EPB   [Adult] Basic Popular Education
               Educación Popular Básica

EPS	Sandinista Army
	Ejército Popular Sandinista
ERET	Rural Work-Study School
	Escuela Rural de Educación Trabajo
FAS	Phonic, Analytical, Synthetic Method
	Método Fónico-Analítico-Sintético
FER	Revolutionary Student Front
	Frente Estudiantil Revolucionario
FP	Preparatory Faculty
	Facultad Preparatoria
FSLN	Sandinista National Liberation Front
	Frente Sandinista de Liberación Nacional
INCAE	Central American Institute of Business Administration
	Instituto Centroamericano de Administración de Empresas
INCINE	The Nicaraguan Film Institute
	El Instituto Nicaragüense de Cine
INNICA	Nicaraguan Institute for the Atlantic Coast
	Instituto Nicaragüense para la Costa Atlantica
INPRHU	Institute for Human Promotion
	Instituto de Promoción Humana
JS-19 J	"19th of July" Sandinista Youth
	Juventud Sandinista "19 de Julio"
LASPAU	Latin American Scholarship Program of American Universities
MECATE	State Movement for Peasant Artistic Expression
	Movimiento de Expresión Campesina Artística Estatal
MED	Ministry of Education
	Ministerio de Educación
MIDINRA	Ministry of Agricultural Development and Land Reform
	Ministerio de Desarrollo Agrícola y Reforma Agraria
MINSA	Ministry of Health
	Ministerio de Salud
MIPLAN	Ministry of Planning
	Ministerio de Planificación
MISURASATA	Miskitu, Sumu, Rama, Sandinistas "All Together"
	Miskitu, Sumu, Rama, Sandinista Asla Takanka
NER	Rural Education Nucleus
	Núcleo Educativo Rural
OAS	Organization of American States
OCIP	Coordinating Organization of Private Institutions
	Organización Coordinadora de Instituciones Privadas
PCD	Democratic Conservative Party
	Partido Conservador Demócrata
PERME	Project for the Elaboration and Reproduction of Educational Materials
	Proyecto de Elaboración y Reproducción de Materiales Educativos
PPSC	Popular Social Christian Party
	Partido Popular Social Cristiano

PRODECO   Program of Communal Educational Development
     Programa de Desarrollo Educativo Comunal
PSC   Social Christian Party
     Partido Social Cristiano
ROCAP   Regional Offices for Central American and Panamanian Affairs
SALA   Southwest Alliance for Latin America
SCIEP   Interamerican Cooperative Service of Public Education
     Servicio Cooperativo Interamericano de Eduación Pública
SINAFORP   National System of Professional Training
     Sistema Nacional de Formación Profesional
SNOT   National System for the Organization of Work
     Sistema Nacional de Organización del Trabajo
TEPCE   Workshop for Educational Evaluation, Programming,
        and Training
     Taller de Evaluación, Programación, y Capacticación Educativa
TM   Middle-Level Degree Technician
     Técnico Medio
TS   High-Level Degree Technician
     Técnico Superior
UAS   Sandinista Literacy Unit
     Unidad Alfabetizadora Sandinista
UCA   Central American University
     Universidad Centroamericana
UNAG   National Union of Farmers and Cattle Ranchers
     Unión Nacional de Agricultores y Ganaderos
UNAN   National Autonomous University
     Universidad Nacional Autónoma de Nicaragua
UNEN   National Union of Nicaraguan Students
     Unión Nacional de Estudiantes Nicaragüenses
UNESCO   United Nations Educational, Social and Cultural Organization
UNI   National Engineering University
     Universidad Nacional de Ingeniería
UPOLI   Polytechnic University
     Universidad Politécnica
USAID   United States Agency for International Development
VIMEDA   Vice-Ministry of Adult Education
     Vice-Ministerio de Educación Adultos

1
Introduction:
The Context and Challenge

   This book examines the role of education in promoting social change in Nicaragua during the first five years of the Sandinista revolution, 1979–84. In Nicaragua, as in other countries undergoing radical change within a socialist framework, education has been called upon 1) to shape a "new person," a more critically conscious and participatory citizen who is motivated by collective ends; and 2) to impart the skills and necessary knowledge to overcome decades of underdevelopment and set the nation on the path of self-sustaining growth.

   The challenges facing the political coalition that came to power in mid-July 1979 were staggering. The Sandinistas inherited a war-torn and economically devastated country. The casualties from the last two years of the struggle to depose the ruling Somoza regime included over 40,000 killed, 100,000 wounded, 40,000 orphaned children, and 200,000 homeless families.[1] The material costs of the war reached $1.8 billion;[2] the gross domestic product had dropped by 25 percent to a level comparable to that of 1962; and the country was heavily indebted. When Anastasio Somoza Debayle fled in July 1979, he left $3.5 million in foreign reserves in the central bank and a deficit of $1.6 billion.

EDUCATION, ECONOMY, AND POLITY
DURING THE SOMOZA PERIOD

   Over the previous three decades, educational expansion and contraction had followed upon booms and busts in the domestic and international economies. In particular, the economic policies of the Somoza regime, in conjunction with international capital, had a profound influence on the content, forms, and scope of educational programs in the country.

During the 1950s and 1960s, the economy had grown at an average annual rate of 5.5 and 6.7 percent respectively.[3] This expansion coincided with the modernization of rural infrastructure to facilitate the export of cotton during the Korean War; the infusion of capital as part of the Alliance for Progress, following the coming to power of Fidel Castro in 1959; and the creation of the Central American Common Market.[4] But in the 1970s, the economy grew at the rate of only 2.2 percent. Among the factors accounting for the downturn were declining terms of trade for raw material exports, exacerbated by the rise in oil prices after 1973; the unbridled rapacity of the Somoza family and the National Guard after the 1972 earthquake, when a substantial portion of international relief aid was misappropriated and, according to Jung, "properly conducted business transactions became impossible";[5] the need to make repayment on the government-based debts (that fueled the industrialization of the 1960s) and the resulting increased taxes on production and consumption;[6] and what Jung has called a "liberal policy of prices, combined with restriction on wages, led from the mid-1970s to an increasing decline in real purchasing power for wage earners. . . ."[7] Real wages of workers in 1974 were 14 percent lower than in 1970, and in 1979, they were equal to those of 1961.[8]

The relatively rapid growth of the economy during the 1950s and 1960s, coupled with substantial foreign aid,[9] had triggered a rapid expansion of schooling. Those reached by primary education programs increased from 68,000 to over 280,000; on the secondary level enrollments grew from approximately 3,600 to over 50,000; and the numbers attending higher education programs grew from under 1,000 to over 9,000. The illiteracy rate had decreased from 63 percent in 1950 to 48 percent in 1971, although in absolute terms there had been an increase from 369,000 to 511,000.

In the 1970s, with the economic downturn, the illiteracy rate again began to rise, the rate of school expansion declined, while the dropout rate increased, and per capita expenditures on secondary and higher education decreased. The sharpest reduction was in higher education allocations, which dropped from $432 per student in 1968, to $294 in 1974.[10]

The education system also was a reflection of the dynastic rule of the Somoza family, in conjunction with the National Guard, which had governed the country either directly or indirectly from the mid-1930s. The overall development policies of the country, according to Petras, might best be described as "rapid growth from above . . . made possible by the autocratic dictatorship and its 'free market' and repressive labor policies—a pattern not unknown to other Latin American countries."[11] He goes on to note that the " 'autocratic development-from-above-and-outside' model prevented sustained and consequential *democratization*. Rather, the pattern was one of selective and time-bound *liberalization*—modification of dictatorial policies—followed by widespread and systematic repression."[12]

Briefly, the so-called "liberal" economic policies of the Somoza family involved capitalization of agriculture for export; concentration of capital and land in fewer, large-scale farming enterprises, which had the effect of driving small owners and tenant farmers off the land and out of subsistence agriculture; limited industrialization, often of a capital-intensive nature, in collaboration with North American and European capital and for domestic luxury consumption or foreign export.

A mass system of public education that would promote the creation of critical, inquiring citizens made little sense in a society characterized by limited opportunity in the modern sector of the economy, and limited opportunity for political participation. The education system reflected these realities.

Educational Underdevelopment

Despite the rhetoric of the Somoza regime, and the 1974 constitution which declared free and compulsory primary education to be a state obligation, the education system in 1979 was extremely underdeveloped and characterized by gross inequities. The illiteracy rate was slightly over half (50.35 percent) of the population with more than three-fourths (76 percent) of rural populations unable to read or write. There were under 25,000 students enrolled in adult education programs, the great majority the responsibility of the private sector and church groups.[13] Primary education reached only 65 percent of the relevant age group; preprimary programs were available to 5.3 percent of children, mostly in private, fee-paying centers; and special education enrolled a mere 355 students.[14] Of those entering the school system, only 22 percent completed the sixth grade—34 percent in urban areas and 6 percent in rural areas. A principal reason for such low completion rates in the countryside was that the vast majority of rural schools consisted of only one or two grades and a single teacher. The following description is typical of educational provision in rural areas in the pre–1979 period.

> Large numbers of pupils never received any instructional materials, and many classrooms were observed that contained up to 90 children, one under-educated teacher, 20 textbooks, one blackboard, and no writing materials to speak of. This in spite of the fact that the U.S. government had donated enough money to provide a textbook for every primary child in all of Central America. Due to the lack of materials, insufficient financial support, and inadequate training, most teachers soon reverted to the traditional lecture-memorization-examination routine, even at the first-grade level.[15]

Only 15 percent of the relevant age group attended secondary education. Approximately 70 percent of secondary schools were private, although they enrolled fewer than half (about 40 percent) of the secondary-school student population. Fees in these schools might be as high as $100 a month, in a country in which, according to Kraft, an estimated 50 percent of the population earned less than $210 per year, and 77 percent of the rural population had never produced annual per capita cash incomes of over $120.[16] With the exception of a few elite private schools and a handful of national institutes receiving USAID support, physical facilities were extremely poor, lacking, in the words of one report, "facilities for good libraries, science laboratories, physical education and other types of special classrooms."[17] In a country in which 45 percent of the population were employed in agriculture and agricultural exports accounted for the lion's share of foreign exchange earnings, less than 1 percent of students were enrolled in agricultural studies, while 87 percent were either in the preuniversity academic program or in commercial studies. The classical secondary school *bachillerato,* which was encyclopedic in nature, as well as verbalistic and memoristic, prepared students for the next step up the educational ladder.[18]

The higher education system, which had expanded considerably during the economic boom years, by the mid-1970s enrolled 5.38 students per 1000 (about 8 percent of the age group).[19] According to the *Encyclopedia of the Third World,* Nicaragua, in 1976, ranked eighty-sixth among nations in adjusted school enrollments for primary and secondary education, but sixty-first in per-capita university enrollments.[20] Like other Latin American countries, Nicaragua under Somoza provided extensive education at public expense to urban elites, but it failed to provide primary education or even basic literacy to a majority of its citizens.[21]

The majority of higher education students were not enrolled in technical fields or careers related directly to production. The private Central American University (*Universidad Centroamericana,* UCA) is a case in point. Although it was established in 1960–61 to meet the need for trained personnel to manage the incipient industrialization occurring in the country,[22] it was nonetheless producing considerably more students for the tertiary or service sectors than for the primary or secondary sectors of the economy, with many students enrolling in business administration and economics.

Overall, more than half of the higher education students in the country were enrolled in courses connected with the tertiary sector while only 2 percent followed courses linked with the primary sector, particularly farming. Of the 27,000 third level students in 1979, for example, only 497 were in agricultural, forestry, and fishery studies, but as many as 4,168 were in commercial and business administration.[23]

In addition to enrollment patterns by field of study, the quality of instruction is an important factor in determining the potential contribution of schooling to the development process. The following information is indicative of the limitations of the pre–1979 school system at all levels. At the higher education level, most teachers were part-time. A number of instructors supplemented their incomes by teaching in high schools, where as many as 68 percent of the teachers were not certified. Going down the line, as many as 73 percent of the primary teachers were unqualified.

The poverty of the country alone does not suffice to explain the underdeveloped state of the education system, which had been shaped and distorted to serve the special interests of the ruling Somoza family and external funders. According to Kraft,

> During the Somoza era, education was seen as a tool to train a technical cadre to run the family enterprises and state bureaucracies, with the emphasis generally in that order. With all important decisions being made by the president, the centralized educational system responded to his general directions. . . . An evidence of the president's interest in education can be seen during the initial days of the reform of the primary education curriculum in the late 1960s, when Somoza went through each curriculum guide prepared by a team of educators and red-penciled-in suggestions and "corrections." The level of interest by the president and the cabinet tended to be in direct proportion to the amount of loans and grants being given by U.S. and international lending agencies which were leading influences over the direction of education in the country.[24]

Dependency

In an interview with the Mexican newspaper *Excelsior,* in 1974, Anastasio Somoza Debayle quipped, "Nicaragua is not a Third World country but a country economically, politically, and militarily dependent on the United States."[25] What Somoza left out was that in addition to its influence on the Nicaraguan polity, economy, and military,[26] the United States also had a major role in shaping the Nicaraguan education system in the areas of curriculum development and implementation, textbooks provision, teacher training, and educational planning.[27]

The first systematic U.S. technical assistance to education began in 1950, at the same time that the Nicaraguan economy was converting to mass-scale cotton production to meet matériel needs of the Korean War. As De Castilla notes, "Thus was initiated the capitalist school of work contrary to the elitist and literary school of the merely agricultural epoch of our economy."[28] A General Agreement of Technical Assistance was signed in December 1950; and in January 1951, the Interamerican Cooperative Service of Public Education (*El Servicio Cooperativo Interamericano de Educación Pública,* SCIEP) was established as part of

President Truman's Point 4 Program. Soon afterwards, projects were initiated for the development of vocational education (June 1951) and the improvement of rural education (February 1952). Among efforts to improve the quality of education in the countryside was the establishment of a rural normal school in Estelí in the early 1960s. Although limited by the general context of underdevelopment and the personalistic politics of the era,[29] it graduated a number of highly qualified educators who came to occupy leadership positions in the post-1979 period.

As noted earlier, USAID placed great emphasis on the production and distribution of school texts. To this end, the Regional Office for Central American and Panamanian affairs (ROCAP) was established. Teams of educators from the United States and the region participated in the elaboration of texts that, despite their high quality, were heavily biased in content and images toward foreign notions of what was appropriate for Nicaraguan children to learn. Moreover, because of corruption and incompetence, many of these books never reached rural schools.[30] Those that did often contained material at a level of sophistication well beyond the competence of many teachers.[31]

The most extensive influence wielded by USAID was in the area of educational planning. In 1969–70, USAID (building on a 1964 report by consultant Grace Scott) funded the Southwest Alliance for Latin America (SALA), a consortium of U.S. universities, to provide technical assistance to the Ministry of Education. SALA, with its headquarters in the Educational Planning Office, helped elaborate, in 1971, the First National Plan for Educational Development 1972–80. Overall, between 1963 and 1972, USAID allocated over $1 million to the rubrics of educational and manpower planning and development,[32] to both strengthen decision-making capabilities of the educational bureaucracy and to produce a school system better designed to meet the so-called "manpower needs" of the economy, shaped in great part by Nicaragua's dependency on the United States for markets and capital.

One critic of U.S. influence on Nicaragua has noted that in many respects that country's education system was a "mirror image of thousands of U.S. school districts."[33] Such an outcome may have been the intention of various outside advisors to the Somoza regime, but this was not possible within the political and economic context of that country.

In many respects, U.S. consultants were attempting to design a system that was more in tune with the educational problems of Nicaragua. A number of USAID missions placed emphasis on rural development, on the contribution of schooling to community improvement, and on education for productive labor. The problem resided precisely in this point: it was outsiders' views of what Nicaragua needed. These views were frequently ethnocentric as well as oblivious to the sociopolitical context of education. That context could not be ignored, nor could the rhetoric of the Somoza regime be accepted uncritically concerning its good intentions—for example, to distribute income more equitably.[34] In 1978, the facts were that the bottom 50 percent of wage earners received only 15 percent of the total income, while the top 20 percent commanded 60 percent.[35] The Somoza family, at the apex of the income pyramid, had amassed a personal fortune of close to $1 billion and owned approximately one-fifth of the country's land and industrial wealth.[36] It is not surprising, therefore, as a 1975 report of the U.S.-based Academy for Educational Development noted, that the Somoza regime had not shown the capacity nor the interest to resolve the problems of the rural poor.[37]

This was the situation facing the new political and educational leadership of the country in 1979. As Minister of Education Carlos Tünnermann Bernheim observed, "On our shoulders we carry a tragic burden."[38] The burden, according to the minister, was that of a primitive and feudal society, a dependent capitalist economy that had failed to develop a progressive and nationalist bourgeoisie, and an entrenched oligarchic and dynastic political system. In contradistinction to this legacy of underdevelopment and dependency, and, in fact, in opposition to it, was another tradition: one of revolutionary struggle and popular education, upon which the post-1979 government was to build.

COUNTERTRADITION: INSURRECTIONAL EDUCATION

This tradition was based on the educational thought and practice of nationalist hero Augusto César Sandino and the Sandinista National Liberation Front (*Frente Sandinista de Liberación Nacional,* FSLN) founder and idealogue Carlos Fonseca Amador. Sandino, in his 1927–33 insurrection against U.S. marine occupation of Nicaragua, had advocated literacy classes for his officers, and an education based on common problems and aimed at improving living conditions. In his essay on the educational thought of Sandino, Tünnermann notes that the first rural school created in Nicaragua beneath the double sign of pedagogy and politics—a school for liberation—was opened by General Sandino in Las Segovias in 1928.[39] In the northern mountains of Nicaragua (which also were to serve as a base for a revolutionary movement against the Somoza regime three decades later), the roles of guerrilla, teacher, and student were all necessarily interchangeable.[40] From that crucible other pedagogical principles emerged: the importance of learning from experience and past errors, the need for theory to guide action, and the collective sharing of knowledge.[41]

Carlos Fonseca Amador, continuing in the tradition of Sandino, exhorted FSLN militants who were organizing combatants, "and also teach them to read." Alongside instruction in weapons, the militants were to teach literacy and raise political consciousness. Novelist and ex-guerrilla commander Omar Cabezas describes the process of political education:

> We would take hold of the campesinos' hands, broad, powerful roughened hands. "These callouses," we asked, "how did you get them?" And they would tell us how they came from the machetes, from working the land. If they got those callouses from working the land, we asked, why did that land belong to the boss and not to them? We were trying to awaken the campesino to his own dream. We wanted to make him see that though the dream was dangerous—since it implied struggle—the land was their right. . . . Through our political work, many campesinos began partaking of that dream.[42]

Similar organizing and educational efforts were undertaken by the National University students. Cabezas, a leader in the Revolutionary Student Front (*Frente Estudiantil Revolucionario,* FER) prior to joining the guerrilla movement in the mountains, notes the process by which FSLN militants raised consciousness in the indigenous Subtiava community of León:

> And we started presenting the image of Sandino in Subtiava. The Indians had a leader, a historical figure, who more than any other was representative of their people: Adiac. We presented Sandino as an incarnation of Adiac, then Adiac as an incarnation of Sandino, but Sandino in the light of the Communist Manifesto, see? So from shack to shack, from Indian to Indian, ideas were circulating: Adiac . . . Sandino . . . class struggle . . . vanguard . . . FSLN.[43]

Similarly, beginning in the 1970s, another group of university students, based primarily at the Central American University, was engaged in community organizing and educational activities in efforts to both topple the Somoza regime and create the foundations for a more just social order. These students based their action not on Marxist notions of class struggle, but on the principles enunciated in the 1968 Conference of Bishops held in Medellin, Colombia, which advocated an institutional preference for the poor and social action to eliminate human suffering and misery.[44] They based their pedagogy on the educational thought of Brazilian educator Paulo Freire, on his notions of adult education as a profoundly political process involving cultural action for freedom.[45] These students, joined by growing segments of parish priests, Catholic orders such as the Jesuits, and a number of Protestant churches (organized in the Evangelical Committee to Promote Development, CEPAD), became active in promoting labor unions, developing skills, and awakening a large number of dispossessed workers and peasants to the possibilities of social change.

Church involvement in social organization and adult education crystallized following the 1972 Managua earthquake which killed over 10,000 and left hundreds of thousands homeless. One of the catalysts for bringing together various groups was the Coordinating Organization of Private Institutions (*Organización Coordinadora de Instituciones Privadas*, OCIP). The various groups brought together by OCIP became involved in discussing the causes of underdevelopment and the importance of education in equipping communities to resolve the problems they faced.[46]

These strands—Sandino's popular national revolt, Marxist class analysis, and Christian Liberation Theology—all came together in the struggle to depose the Somoza regime. The need for self-help and learning from one another, inventiveness in the use of local materials, the value of mass organization and collective action were all lessons derived from the revolutionary movement. For this reason, it is not uncommon to hear current Nicaraguan political leaders and educators articulating the view that the revolution was the greatest teacher of all, and that the continuing revolutionary struggles constitute an enormous school of experience for all.

FSLN's HISTORIC PROGRAM

By the time the FSLN triumphed in July 1979, they already had articulated broad educational goals. As early as 1969, the FSLN, in Chapter 3 of its Historic Program, had articulated its intention to "push forward a massive campaign to immediately wipe out illiteracy," develop national culture, and promote university reform.[47] In 1978, the FSLN issued a 25-point umbrella program under which opponents of the Somoza government could unite.[48] Following the statement of proposals to undertake an agrarian reform, improve working conditions in the mines and cities, promote free unionization of all workers, provide efficient transportation and extend public utilities, construct low-cost and decent housing, initiate public health campaigns and provide basic coverage to all people, Point 14 of the declaration states:

> The Frente Sandinista will dedicate itself from the very start to fight against illiteracy so that all Nicaraguans may learn how to read and write; and everyone, including adults, will be able to attend school to prepare for a career and to excel.
>
> The greater part of the budget will be dedicated to education which will be free of charge and obligatory for all, including high school, and all of the country's schools will be public.
>
> The Sandinista government will struggle together with the people to erect schools everywhere—good schools—and the children will no longer be crowded into tiny rooms with only the floor to sit on.[49]

With the change of government would come a new set of goals for education. If, during the previous four decades of rule by the Somoza family, education was an agency for the maintenance of the status quo, it was, in the post-Somoza era, to contribute to the process of social transformation.[50] In the words of the minister of education, "In accomplishing the Historic Program of the FSLN and the Government Plan of the Junta . . . of National Reconstruction we fight to eradicate ignorance and offer more and better education to our children and youth, because we consider that only an educated citizenry, technically and scientifically prepared, conscious of its responsibilities and rights and disposed to defend the country, can guarantee the success of our revolutionary project."[51]

If Nicaragua, under the Somoza family, could be characterized as an underdeveloped and dependent capitalist society,[52] the new regime quickly delineated a different path to development. According to Miller,

> Concerned with more than simply equity with growth, the leaders of the *Frente Sandinista* shared a general development orientation that was socialist in character. Although interpretations of the precise meaning of this orientation were rich in variety and number, FSLN members did agree on certain common points. Development and transformation, they believed, depended in the short run on national reconstruction and in the long run on a transition to socialism. . . . According to their view, attainment of such a society required economic growth, extensive redistribution of power and wealth, and broad-based citizen participation.[53]

Congruent with this model of development, the new guidelines of educational policy set forth these principles:

● The emergence of the great majority of the people, formerly dispossessed and socially excluded, as the active protagonists of their own education.
● The elimination of illiteracy and the introduction of adult education as priority tasks of the Revolution.
● The linking of the educational process with creative and productive work as an educational principle, leading to educational innovation and promoting the scientific and technical fields.
● The transformation and re-alignment of the education system as a whole, so as to bring it into line with the new economic and social model.[54]

CONTENT AND METHOD OF STUDY

The following chapters explore the challenges, achievements, problems, and contradictions involved in educational expansion and reform during the period 1979–84. Chapter 2 addresses the National Literacy

Crusade of 1980, the first mass-scale undertaking of the new political regime in education. Chapter 3 discusses the follow-up efforts to the literacy campaign—adult basic and nonformal education programs conducted in the community and workplace. Chapter 4 examines quantitative and qualitative changes in preuniversity education. while Chapter 5 describes and analyzes higher education since 1979. Chapter 6 presents concluding remarks.

Throughout the discussion of education and revolution, in Nicaragua, attention is given to the context in which decisions about educational planning and funding are made. Policy makers face many problems, and their options are circumscribed by both the country's past and present realities. Among the ever present constraints and conditions influencing educational decision making are the legacy of underdevelopment, Nicaragua's feudal and dynastic past, and the strategic position of the country between North and South America, which has prompted the United States to interfere in its internal affairs from as early as 1850.[55] It is impossible to understand the current situation in Nicaragua, in society and schooling, without also examining the consequences of present U.S. government hostility toward the Sandinista government. Throughout the discussion references will be made to the impact of U.S. foreign policy on educational development—as well as stagnation—in Nicaragua.

Throughout the study, attention is also given to contradictions that arise in the process of decision making and policy implementation. These contradictions are a concomitant part and consequence of radical change. A focus on contradictions provides a valuable perspective on the dynamics of change and the possibility of social advancement, even while setbacks are encountered.

The material for this book was gathered over a four-year period: beginning in July-August 1980, during the final month of the National Literacy Crusade; in November 1981, as part of a follow-up study of the literacy campaign and an examination of adult education programs; and May-June 1984. The 1984 visit was specifically aimed at gathering material for this book. During the two-month period, over 75 educational decision makers from diverse ministries, public and private agencies, and mass organizations were interveiwed, and visits were made to a variety of schools and educational programs. Secondary data were gathered primarily from different offices of the Ministry of Education, which was also the focus of a majority of interviews, and the National University Council. Although the lion's share of material for this study was gathered in and around Managua, visits were made principally to León, Granada, Estelí, Jinotega, Rama, and Puerto Cabezas, with several of these cities visited on multiple occasions.

Ideally, the study would have been strengthened by a more extended stay in the country and by more systematic observations of a representative sample of schools, classrooms, and community education centers. Excellent first-hand accounts are provided by North American researchers who were directly involved in the educational changes occurring in the country, particularly in the literacy campaign.[56] By comparison, this book endeavors to provide a more comprehensive and possibly more dispassionate overview of different levels of the formal school system as well as different nonformal, or popular, education programs. Emphasis is placed on the word "endeavors" because it is difficult to provide a complete overview of so broad and multifaceted a subject, and because it is difficult to be dispassionate about such undertakings as the 1980 literacy mobilization. Provisos aside, as the story of the Nicaraguan revolution unfolds, with its complexities and contradictions, there is increasingly fertile ground for critical analysis and insight into the limitations as well as potential of education to contribute to social change.

NOTES

1. These data are cited from the Fact Sheet of the Center for International Policy, "The Impact of Civil War in Nicaragua," (Center for International Policy, Washington, D.C., mimeographed, n.d.).

2. Ibid. Included in the costs were $581 million in physical damage, $630 million in revenues lost due to a reduction of the gross domestic product, and $600 million of losses in foreign exchange reserves due to capital flight and illicit withdrawals.

3. Mariano Vargas Narváez, "Situación Socio-Económica y Educación Superior Antes y Después del Triunfo de la Revolución Popular Sandinista" (Concejo Nacional de Educación Superior, CNES, Managua, May 1983, mimeographed) p. 11; and James Petras, "Whither the Nicaraguan Revolution," *Monthly Review* 31 (October 1979): 3.

4. Ibid., 7; and Miguel de Castilla, *Educación y Lucha de Clases en Nicaragua* (Managua: Departamento de Filosofía, Universidad Centroamericana, 1980), pp. 40, 91–100.

5. Harald Jung, "Behind the Nicaraguan Revolution," *New Left Review* 117 (September–October 1979): 76.

6. Ibid.

7. Ibid., 9–10.

8. Vargas, "Situación Socio-Económica," p. 11.

9. On U.S. foreign aid to Nicaragua, see "A Summary History of Thirty-Five Years of U.S. Government Cooperation in Nicaraguan Socio-Economic Development (1942–77)," prepared by H. Bustamente (United States Embassy, USAID, Managua, November 1977); and De Castilla, *Lucha de Clases,* pp. 39–40, 108–13. Also De Castilla's, *La Educación en Nicaragua: Un Caso de Educación para el Desarrollo de Subdesarrollo,* National Seminar on Education in Nicaragua, organized by the Institute for Human Promotion (Managua: Instituto de la Promoción Humana, INPRHU, 1976), pp. 34–56.

10. Richard J. Kraft, "Nicaragua: Educational Opportunity under Pre- and Post-Revolutionary Conditions," in *Politics and Education: Cases from Eleven Nations,* ed. R. Murray Thomas (New York: Pergamon Press, 1983), p. 92.

11. Petras, "Whither the Revolution?" p. 3.

12. Ibid., p. 4.

13. Edgar Macías Gómez, "Análisis de la Estructura y Funcionamiento del Sistema Nacional de Educación de Adultos," in *Educación y Dependencia,* ed. INPRHU (Managua: Instituto de Promoción Humana, 1976), p. 184.

14. MED, "La Gestión Educativa en Cinco Años de Revolución," (Ministry of Education, Managua, May 1984), pp. 1, 19–20, and table A–1.

15. Kraft, "Nicaragua," p. 91.

16. Ibid., p. 89.

17. Jader Habed López and Mario Trana Matus, *La Educación en Nicaragua* (Managua: Division of Human Resources, Ministry of Public Education, 1964), p. 31. For an earlier report on the condition of classrooms and schools, see Cameron D. Ebaugh, *Education in Nicaragua,* Bulletin Number 6 (Washington, D.C.: U.S. Government Printing Office, Superintendent of Documents, 1947), p. 11.

18. Guillermo Rosales Herrera, *"Analisis de la Estructura y Funcionamiento de la Administración del Sistema Educativo Nicaragüense a Nivel Oficial,"* in *Educación y Dependencia,* p. 76.

19. *Encyclopedia of the Third World,* ed. George Thomas Kurian (New York: Facts on File, 1978), 2:1065.

20. Ibid.

21. See, for example, Robert F. Arnove, Michael Chiappetta, and Sylvia Stalker, "Latin American Education," in *Latin America and Caribbean Contemporary Record,* ed. Jack W. Hopkins (New York: Holmes & Meier, 1986).

22. Another reason for establishing the Central American University was the desire of Nicaraguan elites to create a less politicized center of higher studies for their offspring.

23. UNESCO, *1983 Statistical Year Book* (Paris: United Nations Educational, Scientific and Cultural Organization, 1983), pp. iii–297.

24. Kraft, "Nicaragua," p. 85.

25. Cited in Eduardo del Río (Rius), *Nicaragua for Beginners* (New York: Writers and Readers Publishing, 1984), p. 95.

26. For further discussion, see Walter LaFeber, *Inevitable Revolutions: The United States and Central America* (New York: W.W. Norton, 1983), pp. 11, 28–31, 46–48, 160–63, 226–41, 293–98; Thomas W. Walker, *Nicaragua: The Land of Sandino* (Boulder, CO: Westview, 1981), pp. 13–24, 40, 107–13; William M. LeoGrande, "The United States and Nicaragua," in *Nicaragua: The First Five Years,* ed. Thomas W. Walker (New York: Praeger, 1985), pp. 447–67; and Richard Millett, *Guardians of the Dynasty* (New York: Orbis Books, 1977).

27. Richard J. Kraft, "Global Survival," in Richard D. Van Scotter, Richard J. Kraft, John D. Haas, *Foundations of Education: Social Perspectives* (Englewood Cliffs, NJ: Prentice-Hall, 1979), p. 362; and De Castilla, "Desarrollo del Subdesarrollo," p. 56.

28. De Castilla, *Lucha de Clases,* p. 95.

29. Many teachers were not employed or denied opportunities to rise in the educational bureaucracy because of their opposition to the Somoza regime. Con-

versely, many unqualified people, because of political favoritism, were awarded teaching and more lucrative administrative posts.

30. Kraft, "Nicaragua," p. 91.

31. Habed and Trana, "Educación en Nicaragua," p. 12.

32. USAID/Bustamente, "Summary History," pp. 14–16.

33. Kraft, "Global Survival," p. 362.

34. Ibid., 357; and Kraft, "Nicaragua," p. 88.

35. UN/ECLA, "Nicaragua: Repercusiones Económicas de los Acontecimientos Políticos Recientes" (Mexico City, August 1979 mimeographed); cited in Vargas, "Situación Socio-Económica," p. 10.

36. See, for example, Rius, *Nicaragua for Beginners,* pp. 91–95.

37. Academy for Educational Development, *Nicaraguan Education Sector Assessment* (Managua and Washington, D.C.: Academy for Educational Development, 1975); cited in De Castilla, "Desarrollo del Subdesarrollo," p. 34.

38. Carlos Tünnermann Bernheim, "Cinco Años de Educación en la Revolución," (Managua: Ministry of Education, June 1984), pp. 2–3.

39. Carlos Tünnermann Bernheim, *Hacia una Nueva Educación* (Managua: Ministry of Education, 1980), p. 73.

40. Ibid., pp. 73–74.

41. Ibid., pp. 64–69; and Juan Bautista Arríen, *Nicaragua: Revolución y Proyecto Educativo* (Managua: Ministry of Education, 1980), pp. 31–45.

42. Omar Cabezas, *Fire from the Mountain* (New York: Crown Publishers, 1985), p. 210, translated from the original novel in Spanish, *La Montaña Es Algo Mas que una Inmensa Estepa Verde,* by Gonzalo Zapata.

43. Ibid., p. 37.

44. For further discussion of Liberation Theology, see Enrique Dussel, *Theology of Liberation* (Maryknoll, NY: Orbis Books, 1976); Claude Geffre and Gustavo Gutiérrez, ed. *The Mystical and Political Dimension of the Christian Faith* (New York: Herder and Herder, 1974); Denis Goulet, *A New Moral Order: Development Ethics and Liberation Theology* (Maryknoll, NY: Orbis Books, 1974); and Harry A. Landsberger, ed. *The Church and Social Change in Latin America* (Notre Dame, IN: University of Notre Dame Press, 1970).

45. Paulo Freire, "The Adult Literacy Process as Cultural Action for Freedom," *Harvard Educational Review* 40 (May 1970): 205–23; and Paulo Freire, *Pedagogy of the Oppressed* (New York: Herder and Herder, 1970).

46. Interview with Norman Borjan, Consejo Ecuménico pro Ayuda Desarrollo, CEPAD, Managua, May 15, 1984.

47. Sandinista National Liberation Front (FSLN), "The Historic Program of the FSLN," in Tomás Borge et al., *Sandinistas Speak* (New York: Pathfinder Press, 1982); cited in *The Nicaragua Reader,* ed. Peter Rosset and John Vandermeer (New York: Pathfinder Press, 1982), p. 142.

48. "Documents: Why the FSLN Struggles in Unity with the People," *Latin American Perspectives* 20 (Winter 1970): 108.

49. Ibid., 111.

50. MED, *La Educación en Cuatro Años* (Managua: Ministry of Education, 1983), pp. 109–10.

51. Ibid., pp. 7–8.

52. See, for example, Bill Williamson, *Education, Social Structure and De-*

velopment: A Comparative Analysis (New York: Holmes & Meier, 1979), pp. 39–41.

53. Valerie Miller, *Between Struggle and Hope: The Nicaraguan Literacy Crusade* (Boulder, CO: Westview Press, 1985), p. 30.

54. UNESCO, *Educational and Cultural Development Project Nicaragua* (Paris: United Nations Educational, Scientific and Cultural Organization, 1983), p. 35.

55. See, for example, Walker, *Land of Sandino,* pp. 13–15; and Rius, *Nicaragua for Beginners,* pp. 23–29; and other works cited in n. 26.

56. For example, Miller, *Nicaraguan Literacy Crusade*; and Sheryl Hirshon, *And Also Teach Them to Read* (Westport, CT: Lawrence Hill, 1983).

2
The National Literacy Campaign of 1980

The first major undertaking in the field of education by the Nicaraguan Government of National Reconstruction was the Great National Literacy Crusade—Heroes and Martyrs of the Revolution. Widely acclaimed as the most important educational event in the history of the country, the crusade was viewed as a second mass uprising—a "cultural insurrection" that was a sequel to the armed struggle against the Somoza family dictatorship.

In mid-July 1979, within 15 days of coming to power, the new government announced that among other sweeping reforms—confiscation of property belonging to the Somoza family and immediate associates, nationalization of the banks and the mining and lumber industries, land reform, the unionization of workers, and the devolution of decision-making power to mass organizations—there would be a national literacy crusade. The literacy campaign initiated on March 23, 1980, was to symbolize more than any other event or process the transformations occurring in Nicaragua in the initial stages of its revolution. To the question, "Why literacy?" the Nicaraguans answer that the high illiteracy rate that characterized the country—and particularly the rural areas where illiteracy ranged from 60 to 90 percent of the population—was an outcome of the feudal system of the Somoza dynasty, one that kept the vast majority of the population ignorant. As the Ministry of Education's description of

Earlier versions of this chapter appeared as "The Nicaraguan National Literacy Crusade of 1980," *Comparative Education Review* 25 (June 1981): 244–59; and "A View from Nicaragua: Literacy Campaigns and the Transformation of Political Culture," in *Latin America and Caribbean Contemporary Record, Vol. 2: 1982–83,* ed. Jack W. Hopkins (New York: Holmes & Meier, 1984), pp. 245–60.

the Great National Literacy Crusade (*Cruzada Nacional de Alfabetización*, CNA) notes, "to carry out a literacy project and consolidate it with a level of education equivalent to the first grades of primary school, is to democratize a society. It gives the popular masses the first instruments needed to develop awareness of their exploitation and to fight for liberation. Therefore, literacy training was something that the dictatorship could not accept without contradicting itself."[1]

Extending education to the vast majority of the people represented symbolically and substantively a conferral of the rights of citizenship. The literacy campaign constituted a fundamental mechanism for integrating the country—rural and urban populations, the middle and lower classes—and for mobilizing the population around a new set of national goals. In the process, the Sandinista political leadership hoped to win over the majority of people to its vision of a society organized according to a different model. While, as Richard Fagen has observed, Nicaragua is not a socialist country, socialism is very much on the historical agenda.[2] At present, the Sandinista government is nationalist, populist, and pluralist.

It is important to note that the masses of people who rose up in arms against Somoza and the National Guard[3] represented all political persuasions. They were not fighting for socialism, but against a corrupt and brutally repressive regime. They fought in the name of heroes such as Augusto César Sandino and Carlos Fonseca Amador, and for the countless Nicaraguans, among them children and adolescents, who had died in the struggle against the ruling elite. They were fighting for a more just social order, yet to be defined.

It therefore was necessary to establish a massive program of education and reeducation in order to transform the political culture of the country, and to inculcate a new set of values based on more egalitarian social relations, cooperative forms of labor, workers' participation in decision making, a sense of sacrifice for others, and international solidarity with the struggles of peoples in other countries for self-determination and justice. According to Gillette, such a program could take the form either of education *for* socialism—that is, schooling, media and mass campaigns to prepare people for new roles and behaviors and outlooks, or the form of education *within* socialism. The latter means, to paraphrase Gillette,[4] placing people, particularly youth, in nonalienating situations where they can engage in socially productive work that contributes to the general welfare and collective advancement. It is an education that puts theory into practice. The mechanism for this engagement of youth, as well as of diverse adult populations, was the literacy campaign. As the national coordinator of the CNA observed, the literacy campaign was, for many youths, the point of entry into the revolution, the first step toward developing their revolutionary consciousness.[5]

This chapter will describe the scope, organization, content, and aftermath of the Nicaraguan National Literacy Crusade of 1980. Special attention will be given to those aspects of the campaign that relate to the goals of integrating previously excluded groups, stimulating and consolidating national unity, strengthening mass organizations, and encouraging widespread participation in decision making by those individuals and collectivities who were previously the objects but not the subjects of history.[6]

SCOPE AND SYMBOLISM

The extent of the mass mobilization was nothing less than incredible. A campaign of this magnitude and brevity had not been undertaken anywhere. To reduce the illiteracy rate from 50 percent to approximately 15 percent within a period of nine months meant that initially almost every person who knew how to read and write would teach those who did not, and moreover, as adult learners gained minimal literacy skills, they would help those who lagged behind.

Only with mass mobilization, with everyone studying, would it have been possible to find adults willing to face the painful, public embarrassment of attempting to write their names on a blackboard. Only with the universal participation of people of all ages would it have been possible for adults over 60 years of age to learn from youngsters of 12 and 13.

A number of the colorful posters and billboards that adorned the landscape captured the spirit and significance of the literacy campaign. One poster stated:

En cada casa una aula.
En cada mesa un pupitre.
En cada Nica un maestro!
(Every home a classroom.
Every table a school desk.
Every Nicaraguan a teacher!)

Another consists of two scenes, the top one depicting armed people in the streets behind barricades fighting against the National Guard; the bottom one a rural thatched-roof hut with a literacy worker, book open, teaching an entire family (mother, father, and children). The captions read, "Yesterday's Struggle" next to the scene of the barricades, and "Today's Struggle" next to the family learning to read and write together.

The imagery and vocabulary of struggle and national war loomed large in the symbolism of the CNA. Just as six victorious guerrilla armies had converged on Managua on July 19, in the wake of Somoza's flight from the country, so on March 24, 1980, six "armies" left Managua to wage war on illiteracy. The six national fronts of the People's Literacy Army consisted of some 55,000 *brigadistas* (literacy workers), mostly high school students, who would live in the rural areas of the country to work with, learn from, and teach the largely illiterate peasantry. The six fronts were divided into "brigades" at the municipal level, and the brigades in turn were divided into "columns" at the hamlet level. The columns had four "squadrons" of 30 *brigadistas* each; the squadrons consisted of youth of the same sex and roughly the same age who often were from the same school.

In the cities, the People's Literacy Teachers (numbering approximately 26,000) comprised a parallel war effort.[7] These teachers included factory and office workers, professionals, housewives, and high school and university students who for health or family reasons could not leave the city. The urban-based teachers taught after work or during their spare time. The usual pattern was two to three hours of instruction a day, Monday through Friday, although during the final stages of the campaign instruction also took place on weekends.

Although no one was officially required or compelled to teach or become a *brigadista,* schools were required to participate, and students who did not join in risked the danger of losing credit for the academic year. Over 250,000 literate youths and adults volunteered to participate in the CNA.[8] At the time, the total populations of Nicaragua was about 2.4 million, of whom 717,000 were at least ten years old and literate.

STRUCTURE OF CNA

The deployment, logistical support, and protection of the literacy army members required the support of every national ministry and mass organization. Literacy workers had to be transported to the remotest corners of the country, often inaccessible by road and four-wheel vehicles;[9] they had to be housed, fed, and safeguarded. The dangers *brigadistas* were exposed to in the countryside reflected not only the ravages of underdevelopment—the lack of potable water, the scarcity of food, and endemic diseases such as dysentery and malaria—but included the imminent threat of terrorist attacks by several thousand ex-guardsmen who had fled to neighboring Honduras and regularly slipped across the border to terrorize and murder *brigadistas* who symbolized the revolutionary changes occurring in Nicaragua. Nine literacy workers were assassinated during different stages of the crusade by counterrevolutionaries known as *contras.* In case of illness or injury there was a need for emergency medical services; and in case of counterrevolutionary attacks, there was a need for a permanent communications network to alert defense officials.

Complementing these efforts to place and support the *brigadistas* were activities to publicize the literacy crusade, identify those who did not know how to read and write, and encourage them to attend literacy units and complete the literacy process.

A National Coordinating Commission was established under the auspices of the Ministry of Education to determine broad policy and facilitate implementation of all these efforts. The commission consisted of 25 ministerial, political, military, educational, cultural, religious, and mass organizations. These included the Ministries of Culture, Interior, Social Welfare, Health, Planning, Transportation, and Public Works; the Institutes of Agrarian Reform and Development; the National Directorate of the FSLN; the Popular Sandinista Army; the Sandinista Defense Committees; the Nicaraguan Women's Association "Luisa Amanda Espinoza"; The Rural Workers' Association; the Sandinista Workers Central; the Sandinista Youth of July 19; the Federation of Secondary Education Students; the National Association of Nicaraguan Educators; the Catholic Church and the Federation of Catholic Teachers; and the two universities—the National Autonomous University and the Central American University. Parallel coordinating commissions for the CNA were established at departmental and municipal levels. According to outside observers, the national and departmental committees were only shadow organizations; it was at the municipal level where the crusade took form, where the participation of the masses was most apparent.[10] And it was the mass organizations that were to play the principal role in implementing the literacy campaign.

MASS ORGANIZATION PARTICIPATION

The mass organizations that were instrumental in overthrowing the dictatorship were the key to the CNA's success. Organizations in Nicaragua had been formed at factory and neighborhood levels by workers, women, and youth; they involved tens of thousands of Nicaraguans who provided supplies to the revolutionary army, set up communication networks, administered first aid, obtained and distributed weapons, and erected barricades to do battle during the uprisings of 1978 and 1979.

Following the victory, these mass organizations, in many cases renamed and reconstituted, took their place in the battle against illiteracy. The Sandinista Workers Central (CST) assumed responsibility for literacy-related activities in factories, forming Workers' Literacy Militias with some 3,000 of its members. Similarly, the Rural Workers' Association (ATC) assumed responsibility for rural areas and recruited a contingent of its affiliates to serve as literacy teachers in Peasant Literacy Militias. In the cities, the Sandinista Defense Committees (CDS) were the major organizing force. Nationwide, the Nicaraguan Women's Association "Luisa Amanda Espinoza" (AMNLAE) mobilized women to participate in the campaign and through various support groups attended to the welfare of the *brigadistas*. Teachers were another group whose participation was essential to the successful implementation of the CNA. Over 9,000 teachers assisted in the preparation, supervision, and in-service training of the literacy workers. Notable among their efforts was the formation of a "red and black flag" brigade to serve in the most remote and dangerous areas of the country. In addition, they helped maintain educational, cultural, and recreational activities for youth while schools were officially closed between March and September; furthermore, they established special educational programs for children who were street vendors. Assisting the National Educators' Association (ANDEN), were university-level school of education majors.

CONTENT AND PEDAGOGY OF LITERACY MATERIALS

Learning activity centered on the basic reader, *Sunrise of the People*.[11] Based in part on the pedagogical ideas of the Brazilian adult educator Paulo Freire, the reader contains 23 generative themes. Each theme, accompanied by a photograph, consists of generative polysyllabic words which can be broken down into basic sound and meaning units (phonemes and morphemes) and recombined by the learner to form new words. The initial themes pertain to the revolutionary heroes Augusto César Sandino and Carlos Fonseca Amador and progressively cover the topics of the struggle for national liberation; the termination of exploitation by foreign and national elites; the role of the mass organizations and the Popular Sandinista Army in defending the revolution; the rights and responsibilities of the citizenry of the new society; the achievements of the Government of National Reconstruction in undertaking land reform and in expanding and extending health care, education, and other social welfare services; the liberation of women from subservient roles; the integration of the long-abandoned Atlantic Coast region into the national society; and, finally, the commitment of the new revolutionary regime to solidarity with other progressive governments of the world.[12] At the core of these themes are emotionally charged phrases and words. Appropriately, the first such word is *revolución*. Pedagogically, the words *la revolución* contain all the vowels of the Spanish alphabet. Other generative words include *liberación, genocidio,* and *masas populares*. To summarize the sequency of pedagogical activity: with the introduction of each photograph there was to be approximately an hour of group discussion, followed by one hour of practice related to reading the text and decoding and encoding the generative words. The format of group discussion, however, was frequently not followed—given the inexperience of the teachers and the reluctance of students to discuss issues publicly or to question authority.

Sheryl Hirshon, a United States teacher who volunteered her services as a supervisor of a group of 25 *brigadistas* in the northern mountainous province of Matagalpa, vividly describes the difficulties of implementing this innovative pedagogy in her book, *And Also Teach Them to Read*. According to Hirshon, the first step of each lesson—the dialogue between the literacy instructors and the adult students—was the most difficult to conduct: "the *brigadistas* found it a frustrating and confusing assignment. What was it for? Certainly *they'd* never been taught that way. In all too many of the classes it was done badly, or ignored altogether."[13]

The CNA endeavored to put into practice a number of Freire's pedagogical concepts, principally those which conceive of adult education as a political process involving consciousness raising, and those which stimulate individuals to see themselves as makers of culture and transformers of their environment. But the CNA also departed in significant ways from Freire's educational model, which stresses the necessity of developing materials in dialogue with the learning community and on the basis of a sociocultural analysis of that community.[14] According to Freire's ideal, literacy workers should not arrive in a community with a prepared text.

Such an approach was not really possible in Nicaragua, where an all-out assault on illiteracy using the volunteer labor of minimally trained and mostly young people could not have been accomplished by strict adherence to Freire's ideal model concerning content development (based on a sociocultural and linguistic analysis of each community of the country).[15] Instead, a primer was developed by a national team of educators in consultation with top political leaders. To the credit of the Nicaraguan campaign, the literacy materials reflect careful pedagogical planning in the selection and sequencing of content. The materials are also based on respect for the experience and social world of the adult learners.[16]

The most common criticisms of the literacy materials focus on their ideological nature. The most vocal opposition was directed at the pro-FSLN content of the literacy crusade. Some of those who object to political propagandizing as part of the literacy process are oblivious to the indoctrination that occurs in all education systems.[17] They fail to see that what differs from one system to another is the subtlety of the indoctrination, the content of the messages, and the sociopolitical purposes of instruction. They see the messages as indoctrination only when they are in conflict with their own personally held convictions or ideology.

To repeat the fundamental question posed by Freire, is the object of a literacy campaign domestication or liberation?[18] Are the educational programs designed to provide limited information so that people can better fit into the existing hierarchical structures and do the bidding of dominant groups?[19] Or is the literacy process designed to provide an indispensable base of knowledge that opens up options for formerly dispossessed people, providing them with the understandings, skills, and attitudinal dispositions that equip them to play a decisive role in forging a new society?

The Government of National Reconstruction posited that under successive regimes of the Somoza dynasty (1937–79), education worked to legitimate an inequitable social order that prepared elite groups for leadership roles while denying fundamental knowledge and skills to the vast majority.[20] In contrast to the passivity and fatalism fostered in the masses by previous regimes, the new Sandinista-led government proposed to instill a different set of values and a radically different ideology. According to the curriculum developers, the materials used in the literacy and postliteracy educational campaigns were designed to prepare people to play an active role in creating a more prosperous and just society. Consonant with the characteristics of the present political leadership of the country, the values of nationalism and populism were stressed; but also emphasized were the values of a country attempting to follow a development model based on collective work efforts, personal sacrifice, and national austerity to create greater abundance.

These are laudable goals. However, it is still open to debate whether the pedagogy actually employed fostered critical consciousness or top-down indoctrination. Hirshon narrates the difficulties involved in depending on poorly prepared and often impatient *brigadistas* to stimulate adult learners to reach the stage of independent thought. The following account is taken from a Saturday workshop in which her group of *brigadistas* discussed common problems and concerns.

> I try to do it [the dialogue] right, but students say "we don't want to talk politics; just get on to the syllables."
>
> May I speak, *profe*? Listen, *compa*.* If your students say that, it's because you've made them feel that it isn't important. If we just come and teach reading, we aren't doing anything. This crusade was planned so that the workers and peasants could really understand the national reality, and if you just teach letters and syllables, you're not even fulfilling your duty as a brigadista.
>
> That's right, Miguel, but you have to be careful about the opposite danger, too, which is that the exercise becomes more important than letting the students know you are really interested in what they have to say. When I saw your class, you started really well, but when people remained shy, you ended up giving a speech. That's when people get the idea it's some kind of political indoctrination.[21]

---

*The word *compa* is a Nicaraguan abbreviated form of the word *compañero*, which may be translated to mean companion or colleague. It is frequently used by people sympathetic to the FSLN, and those who participated in the insurrection against Somoza or who are involved in joint efforts related to national reconstruction.

Low-income and rural populations reached by the literacy campaign had traditionally been excluded from participation in decision making; they had been taught to defer to authority, to be mute and passive. When they spoke out and challenged authority, the response almost always had been punitive. Thus it was not uncommon to find that rural people felt uncomfortable discussing their opinions publicly or questioning authority—although that authority might be an adolescent teacher some 20 or 30 years their junior. Asking these learners to be active participants in their own education directly opposed ingrained traditions of subordination and self-deprecation. Taking into account these dispositions on the part of the learners, as well as the inexperience of the youthful instructors, it is not surprising that the CNA, in its final stages, resembled a traditional teacher-directed pedagogy and an almost mechanical approach to literacy instruction. What was supposed to be dialogue often consisted of the literacy worker merely reading notes jotted down from the teacher's guide. The national campaign goal was to have a certain number of learners reach lesson 23 and successfully pass the five-part literacy test by mid-August. As this deadline approached, the literacy workers increasingly concentrated on rote drill of phonic sequences (such as pri, pre, pra, pro, pru/ gri, gre, gra, gro, gru). Despite the political consciousness-raising objectives of the campaign, it should have been obvious to anyone observing classes that many learners were essentially grappling with letters, sounds, parts, and blocks of words—not ideas.

It is possible, however, that the most important political lessons of the crusade resided not in the literacy materials or the teacher-learner encounters, but in the very existence of the campaign itself. The literacy crusade was a symbol of justice, of the concern of the new political regime for the most neglected areas and populations of the country. It involved the extension of national authority and services into previously unreached corners of the society. The commitment of the revolutionary Sandinista regime was most palpably present in the *brigadistas* who went to live with and assist impoverished rural families, and in the "urban literacy guerrillas" who worked in the poorest *barrios* of Managua and other cities. Thus, in studying the political impact of the CNA, it may be more enlightening to study the overall process, structure, and context of learning rather than the explicit content of instruction.

FOLLOW-UP CAMPAIGN IN INDIGENOUS LANGUAGES

Immediately following the termination of the National Literacy Crusade on August 23, the government began preparing for a campaign in the three major indigenous languages of the Atlantic Coast region of Nicaragua—English, Miskito, and Sumo. Geographically, historically, and culturally, the Atlantic Coast has always constituted a distinct and distant population, tenuously integrated with the spanish-speaking Pacific Coast region.[22] The Atlantic Coast region contains approximately 50 percent of the territory of Nicaragua, but only about 10 percent of its population. In large expanses of the East Coast—along the Río Coco and in the areas of Puerto Cabezas and Bluefields—the majority of the inhabitants speak either Miskito or Creole/English as their native tongue. In scattered pockets along the coast between 2 and 5 percent speak Sumo, Rama, and Carib. Many of the coastal peoples, however, speak two or three languages (principally, Spanish, English, and Miskito)[23] with varying degrees of fluency, switching back and forth between them depending on the language situation.

According to the October 1979 census (88,389 people or) 75 percent of the region's population ten years of age and older were illiterate.[24] Between March and August 1980, approximately 50,000 coastal people (*costeños*) participated in the Spanish-language literacy crusade, reducing illiteracy to about 30 percent of the inhabitants of the coastal departments of Puerto Cabezas, Bluefields, and Rama. Many of the indigenous-speaking people who opted to acquire literacy in Spanish did so in order to participate in national institutions and communicate with the rest of the country. It also appears that the more pro-Sandinista inhabitants were those who sought literacy in Spanish.

By the end of the National Literacy Crusade, there were still a substantial number of *costeños* who were illiterate and who preferred to participate in literacy classes conducted in English, Miskito, and Sumo.[25] Over 12,500 people participated in and completed the indigenous campaign, which took place between October 1980 and March 1981. With the completion of this campaign, illiteracy had been reduced to approximately 22 percent of the Atlantic Coast population.

In the aftermath of the crusade (CNA) and the campaign in languages, students, both young and old, entered the new system of Adult Basic Education (EPB), which was placed under a newly established Vice-Ministry of Adult Education (VIMEDA). The core of this system—which will be discussed at greater length in Chapter 3—consists of Basic Education Collectives (*Collectivos de Educación Popular*, CEPs), in which the sole language of instruction is Spanish. The Vice-Ministry of Adult Education has taken the position that knowledge of Spanish is essential to unify the country, and that it would be neither feasible nor desirable to erect a parallel system of instruction in a second or third language. Since achievement of national unity was one of the principal goals of the CNA, it is to this objective as well as other outcomes that the discussion now turns.

OUTCOMES

The outcomes of the CNA may be studied at various levels. The most obvious results are found in the number of adult learners who passed the literacy test or completed a certain number of lessons in the primer. Observers may also point to the physical improvements in communities where literacy workers resided.[26] At a more profound level, the outcomes of the CNA must be evaluated in relation to the transformation of political culture, the integration of previously alienated sectors of the country, the unification of countryside and city as well as the Pacific and Atlantic Coast regions, the winning of youth to the revolution, the improvement of the status of women in Nicaraguan society, and the strengthening of mass organizations. All of these were important political priorities of the revolutionary Sandinista government.

Literacy Achievements

In the history of twentieth century literacy campaigns, three cases stand out as truly remarkable achievements. In 1970, Tanzania mobilized its population around the theme of adult education; literacy classes sprang up all over the country—in schools, churches, factories, and fields; and by 1977, the illiteracy rate had been reduced from 67 percent to 27 percent.[27] On April 15, 1961, Cuba declared a national war on illiteracy; by the end of that year illiteracy had been reduced from 23.6 percent[28] to 3.9 percent of the adult population of four million. Thus, within two years of the revolution that toppled Fulgencio Batista and brought Fidel Castro to power, Cuba became the first country in Latin America to claim that it had eliminated illiteracy. Even more impressive, and perhaps the single most impressive undertaking in the field of literacy campaigns, is that of Nicaragua. Mounted within the first year of a revolutionary regime, the campaign was able to reduce the illiteracy rate from 50.35 percent (N = 722,616) of the population over the age of ten to approximately 23 percent in five months. Campaign officials have claimed that the illiteracy rate had been reduced to 12.96 percent; but it should be noted that this lower figure is based on the government's decision to subtract from the target population of illiterate adults approximately 130,000 individuals who were considered unteachable or learning impaired. These were people who because of blindness, debilitating illnesses, advanced age, senility, or institutionalization were not able to participate in the literacy campaign. Whether the higher figure of 23 percent or the Nicaraguan official claim of 12.9 percent is accepted as the illiteracy rate, the accomplishments of the CNA were singularly impressive. Between March 23 and August 23, 1980, a total of 406,056 Nicaraguans had learned to read and write. This achievement occurred in a war-torn and economically devastated country. In addition, the campaign in languages on the Atlantic Coast extended literacy skills to another 12,664. Despite attempts by critics to discredit the level of literacy achieved during the five-month campaign, and despite claims that there are people who have literacy certificates who cannot read a single word on their diplomas,[29] the general consensus of independent observers is that there was a systematic effort to assure that the adult students had achieved certifiable literacy skills. The five-part final examination consisted of the learners writing their names, reading a paragraph containing vocabulary from the more advanced lessons (roughly equivalent to a third grade primary education text), answering questions about the paragraph, taking dictation on the paragraph, and writing their thoughts on one of three themes (for example, what the Sandinista revolution meant to them).

Achieving this level of competency, however, was just the beginning of a process of continuing adult education. At the same time, educational opportunity was to be provided to 46,600 participants in the CNA who at the end of the official campaign in mid-August 1980 had not completed the literacy primer and therefore were considered to be semi-literate. It was to be provided as well to those illiterate adults who, for a variety of reasons, were not able to participate in the CNA. Continuing adult education programs will be discussed in Chapter 3.

In recognition of these achievements in the field of literacy, UNESCO selected Nicaragua as the recipient of the Nadezhda K. Krupskaya Award in September 1980. The international jury cited not only the magnitude of the literacy project in Nicaragua, but also the fact that the Nicaraguan government had given priority to general literacy as a fundamental component of the process of national reconstruction. The jury further recognized that the campaign "offered an enduring testimony to the nobility of human spirit thanks to the exemplary dedication of the voluntary teachers of whom more than fifty gave their lives to the service of their compatriots."[30]

Engagement of Youth: Raising
Consciousness and Commitment

Although a majority of the combatants against Somoza were under 25 years of age,[31] many youths did not participate in the armed struggle.

However, the literacy crusade provided them (as well as other groups such as teachers) an opportunity to play an active part in the process of national reconstruction. Approximately 20,000 youths were involved in the final stages of the general insurrection against the deposed regime; 65,000 youths were involved in the CNA.[32] Their participation in the campaign changed their status from marginal to being engaged in national life (in fact, young people were considered by Anstasio Somoza Debayle and the National Guard to be public enemies), to being key actors in the creation of a new society. As a result of their involvement in the CNA, many youths were to undergo substantial transformations in their values and in their perceptions of themselves and their place in national society.

Although they were sent to the countryside as teachers, the *brigadistas* were also cast in the role of learners—placed in an unfamiliar world far distant from the comfortable middle-class existence most knew. As Don José, a recently literate peasant farmer, wrote to the mother of his literacy worker,

> Do you know I'm not ignorant anymore? I know how to read now. Not perfectly, you understand, but I know how. And do you know, your son isn't ignorant anymore either. Now he knows how we live, what we eat, how we work, and he knows the life of the mountains. Your son, ma'am, has learned to read from our book.[33]

Beverly Treumann, one of a handful of United States citizens who served as a volunteer in the CNA, provides an account of the metamorphosis in her middle-class friend Julia: Before becoming a *brigadista,* Julia had described herself as a snob who would not greet the *campesinos* (peasant farmers) who came into town, who fussed a lot about dressing up and putting on make-up, and who filed and painted her toenails. But according to Treumann's account,

> Julia now (at the end of the campaign) knows personally how most Nicaraguans live. She spent five months eating beans and tortillas, sleeping with fleas, getting up at 4 A.M., sharing a bedroom with a whole family, hiking for miles through mud and rock without the convenience of even an outhouse. She knows lots of once-illiterate people whom she regards as far more talented and intelligent than herself [the members of her peasant family].[34]

As the then Minister of Education, Carlos Tünnermann Bernheim, noted, "The CNA was a great school for the brigade members; one often asks oneself: who learned more, the literacy-teachers from the peasants or the peasants from the literacy teachers? Many literacy-teachers have said they thought it was actually they who learned more during their stay in the countryside. . . ."[35]

The most striking evidence of these changes in youth are found in personal histories. Learning about the countryside was stimulated by the requirement that all *brigadistas* keep a diary. The diary, as outlined by the CNA administration, was to include a detailed description of all major aspects of the community in which the volunteer resided: the history of the community, physical features, principal economic activities, social agencies, developmental activities undertaken, and so forth. In addition, cultural brigades consisting of some 450 students organized by the Ministry of Culture and the National University gathered systematic data on archaeological sites, folk traditions, artisan activities, and, in general, compiled an oral history of the popular insurrection against the Somoza regime.

Beyond the intimate learning about rural conditions that was to take place, the other major change that the *brigadistas* describe is a great gain in self-confidence and a resolve to work wherever they are needed by the revolution. Treumann ends her account of Julia this way: "Julia, who had once viewed the crusade as a five-month act of routine patriotism after which life would return to its normal worries, has become courageous and self-sacrificing.[36]

As Carlos Carrión, head of the CNA general staff, has noted, "the youth of the country don't have to convince themselves that they can play a role in society. They have already proven it."[37]

Following the literacy campaign, many of the *brigadistas* continued their active involvement in the Sandinista Youth Organization (*Juventud Sandinistas* 19 *de Julio*—JS–19 J), participating in militia service and health campaigns, and contributing voluntary labor for different crop harvests. For example, in 1983, over 20,000 students participated in volunteer production brigades (BEP) to help with the coffee and cotton harvests. Over 36.4 percent of the members of the Managua militia were students, 15 percent of students participated in military defense, and some 27,000 students participated in civil defense.[38] Students (many of whom are ex-*brigadistas*) also comprise a majority of the over 80,000 people who have been involved in health mobilizations to immunize the population against polio, malaria, and other major diseases. Besides these indicators of the commitment of youth to participate in the tasks of national reconstruction, data are available on the impact of the CNA on the political consciousness of young literacy workers. In what is perhaps the only study of this kind undertaken in Nicaragua to date, Flora, McFadden, and Warner surveyed 1,079 third-year high school students from Managua, Estelí (Nicaragua's fourth largest city), and the rural community of San Rafael in the department of Jinotega. The sample consisted of *brigadistas*, urban literacy workers who lived at home during the CNA, and a control group of students who did not participate in the campaign.[39] The researchers conclude that "the national literacy crusade, in spite of problems in recruitment, training, and logistics arising from the rapidity with which the campaign was put together and from the fact the bourgeois *brigadistas* were often supervised by conservative teachers, had a positive impact on the young participants which was independent of their involvement in the insurrection. Those who did not participate in the insurrection showed greater growth in support for the revolution than those who did."[40] Although the researchers found that "working-class students are more committed to the revolution in word and deed than are their higher class companions, participation in the crusade was associated more strongly with subsequent revolutionary attitudes and activities for middle- and upper-class students than for working-class students."[41]

Participation in the crusade, however, was not always associated with an increase in support for the revolution. For 13 percent of the *brigadistas* in the above study, participation in the CNA was cited as the determining factor in decreasing revolutionary support.[42]

Ambiguous and even contradictory outcomes of involvement in the CNA may be a consequence of individuals' past biographies and class positions as well as changing opportunity structures within the country. For example, returning one year after the termination of the literacy campaign, Treumann once again observed Julia:

> Julia was a different story. She continues to volunteer for such things as health brigades and coffee harvesting, but when I asked about the revolution she wrinkled her nose, smiled and said she was "contra"—short for counter revolutionary. "She's joking," said a friend of hers, but I didn't think it was wholly a joke. And yet, when I asked her about her future, she said she wants to become an agronomist—an intriguing career choice much favored by the revolution; no other change could put her closer to the heart of the important social change. Her father frowns on it: "Not a good choice for a woman." But her boyfriend not only approves but would like to study also.[43]

It would be difficult to speak of a new Nicaraguan person characterized by such values as altruism and a willingness to sacrifice for others. However, the literacy crusade provided an opportunity for many youths to put into practice such values and to demonstrate a maturity that far exceeded their years. Hirshon has said that for many of the city-bred youths, the rural experience with the CNA represented "a move from intellectual to physical and emotional commitment. Fighting for an abstract idea wasn't the same as fighting for a lived conviction."[44] Among the abstractions to take on concrete meaning for *brigadistas* were the *campesinos* with whom they lived.

But also for the *campesinos* a number of abstractions also were to acquire intimate meaning. The changes in the rural populations, the raising of consciousness and participatory levels of peasant farmers, as well as the linking-up of countryside and city, is the next topic of analysis.

**Integration of Rural Populations
into National Life**

According to Hirshon, "The literacy crusade had been basically conceived as a dialectic—a meeting of opposites: city kids with country
people, intellectual with manual work, independence with discipline,
traditional thought patterns with revolutionary new ideas."[45] The
crusade also has been described by a distinguished Nicaraguan poet as a
national *entrevivencia,* a coming together and sharing of living experiences of urban and rural populations.[46] The encounters of these two distinct worlds was to engender mutual respect and understanding as well as
more egalitarian social relations. The gain in self-confidence reported by
so many literacy workers was matched by similar developments in many of
the peasant farmers who learned more than just to read and write during
the crusade. Previously self-deprecating before city people, especially
those who might have a secondary or higher education, they were now
more assertive. As Anita Mikkonen, an international volunteer from Fin-
land, observed, "During the Literacy Campaign, the [rural] adults enormously expanded their view of the world and became more self-confi-
dent; instead of being the forgotten part of the population they were beginning to realize that they were the protagonists of a gigantic national
effort."[47]

The involvement of the newly literate peasants in the tasks of national
reconstruction is manifest in a variety of ways, including membership in
farming cooperatives and workers associations, and participation in rural
militias. Perhaps the best indicator of their heightened commitment is the
fact that they comprise the bulk of instructors in over 17,000 adult education collectives formed in the aftermath of the CNA.

More than commitments were awakened by the CNA. The crusade
also contributed to expectations of expanded national services in previously neglected areas such as health and to demands for consumer products that were unfamiliar to most rural households prior to the arrival of
the *brigadistas.* The *brigadistas* were provided with two rations of basic
food commodities to feed themselves and to assist their host families.
Moreover, as Cardenal and Miller note, "Weekend visits by parents and
care packages from home helped improve the community diet."[48] One
unforeseen result of the CNA was a tremendous—and inflationary—increase in the rural demand for such products as refined sugar, salt, cooking oil, and poultry products.

While the *brigadistas* were expanding the horizons of rural populations, it is also the case that urban populations were discovering at first
hand the countryside. According to the mother of three literacy teachers,
"The Literacy Crusade taught us two things. One, what our children are
capable of doing and of becoming. Two, what our country is like and how
gentle and how poor our people are in the countryside."[49] Not only the

brigadistas but thousands of middle-class parents who were to visit their children during the crusade gained an appreciation of the *campesinos,* who are now considered family members. It is not uncommon for the *brigadistas,* for example, to refer to their hosts as their *campesino* mother or father. It is also quite common to see at holiday time, particularly Christmas, thousands of former literacy workers boarding buses in the cities on their way to visit their *campesino* families.

To conclude this section, the CNA played a critical role in helping to liberate rural populations from their previous isolation and neglect; and it initiated the long-term process of integrating the rural sector into national development efforts. The aroused political consciousness of the peasantry went hand in hand with the acquisition of literacy skills and the opening of economic opportunities with large-scale agrarian reform. In turn, the economic and social transformation occurring in the rural areas since 1979 were to place increasingly greater demands on rural farmers and workers for more sophisticated technical skills and knowledge.

Improving the Status of Women

Among the other changes that were to be accelerated and magnified by the CNA was the liberation of women from their marginal positions in society. During the large-scale fighting of 1978–79, women not only formed support groups, but played an active role in combat, comprising up to one-third of some guerrilla units—and in the case of León, five women were in command of the capture and running of the city.[50]

The literacy crusade brought even more women into important public roles. It has been described as the first national task in which women had equal participation.[51] By far the most educationally neglected group in the country, women seized the opportunity to teach and study during the crusade—the CNA was to be their own personal vindication of past abandonment and subordination. During the CNA, women comprised the majority of teachers (60 percent) and technical personnel. In the follow-up adult education programs, they comprise approximately 46 percent of the students and instructional personnel.

As with the mobilization of youth, once women were engaged in the process of national transformation through new teaching-learning roles, they became available for a variety of other tasks such as militia duty and voluntary participation in agricultural production. In 1983, for example, women comprised 80 percent of the over 70,000 health *brigadistas* involved in immunization campaigns, and 75 percent of the nearly 9,000 health workers in the country. Women also represent 48 percent of militia members, and 60 percent of those involved in revolutionary vigilance (night time guarding of public property against sabotage by counterrevolutionary forces).[52] Militancy is reflected in the notion expressed by a member of the national executive committee of the national women's association (AMNLAE) that the revolution in and of itself does not resolve any problems for women; the revolution merely provides opportunities for women to begin to redress their grievances and to achieve more equal status. And it is women themselves who must take the initiative to win their rights.[53]

At the same time, the Sandinista government, with the prompting and support of AMNLAE, has instituted a number of positive policies to both expand job opportunities for women and end past practices that involved the commercial exploitation of women.[54] AMNLAE itself, as a mass organization with representation on the Council of State (1980–84), played a leading role in introducing legislation to protect the rights of women and to ensure male sharing of responsibility for household chores.[55]

These laws articulate ideals yet to be achieved, but as statements of public policy they are nonetheless important. It is unrealistic to expect that traditional sex role perceptions and modes of interaction will completely change within a span of five years. Indeed, the high incidence of reported divorces and separations attests to the tensions that accompany such changes.

The AMNLAE statement, "Women's Participation in the New Nicaragua," summarizes the current situation: "*Machismo*, as part of the heritage of a society based on exploitation, still persists in many men and women. Unfortunately, it is much easier to destroy oppressive and repressive political and economic structures than the people's mental structures. . . . Nicaraguan women are fully convinced that women will be free to the extent that both men and women become free: that liberty is not granted but won."[56]

Strengthening Mass Organizations

Another significant outcome of the CNA was the strengthening of mass organizations as valid and effective vehicles of popular participation in the postwar period of reconstruction. The continued democratization of post-Somoza Nicaragua depends on the vitality and expansion of these organizations. In the context of Nicaragua's poverty, these organizations play a further critical role in mobilizing people to contribute voluntary labor and in stimulating workers to higher levels of productivity.

At the beginning of the crusade, many of the mass organizations were in a fledgling state. As Treumann notes,

We [the *brigadistas*] brought organization and more services. The *campesinos* had organized to receive us and part of our work was to help those first committees expand into community organizations, farmworkers' associations, women's groups and the people's militias. Or, as the members of these groups now like to say, it was during the literacy crusade they "put in the batteries" and got going.[57]

As a case in point, before 1979 the Rural Workers' Association (ATC) only had organizational influence in the four different departments of Managua, Carazo, Rivas, and Chinandenga. By 1980, the association had more than doubled its membership to well over 100,000 affiliates. The ATC, which helped recruit *milicianas campesinos de alfabetización* (peasant literacy militias), was able to use the CNA as a vehicle for unionizing rural workers and helping farmers to organize into cooperatives.[58]

The National Educators' Association (ANDEN) gained new strength and an enhanced self-image through its participation in the crusade. It was the vehicle for mobilizing teachers. As with students and women, the CNA provided the first major opportunity for teachers to become involved on a massive scale in revolutionary activities. Teachers, as an occupational group, had suffered political repression under the outgoing Somoza regime, which prevented them from unionizing and which used all the powers at its command to punish militant teachers and reward loyal servants. Many members of the teaching force, therefore, were either politically apathetic or acquiescent. According to Nubia Pallavaccini of the national executive committee of ANDEN, the crusade made teachers feel once again that they had much to give.[59] Their participation as trainers and supervisors in the countryside and cities was to help overcome the gulf—if not the hostility—that existed between them and many of the youths who had participated in the rural guerrilla struggle or the urban insurrections. These youths were often contemptuous of their teachers whom they considered collaborators with the old system or cowardly in their character.

Teachers and their association, ANDEN, have since moved into a key role in revolutionary Nicaragua. Along with the Nicaraguan Women's Association, the Rural Workers' Association, the Sandinista Workers' Confederation (CST), and the Sandinista Defense Committees (CDS), ANDEN has achieved the status of a mass organization that has had formal representation on the Council of State and has been consulted by the Sandinista government in all matters pertaining to the field of education, the care and protection of youth, and national defense. ANDEN also sits on the National Education Council of the government and the national advisory councils of the Ministry of Education, the Vice-Ministry of Adult Education, and the Ministry of Health (for programs in "popular health").

The Sandinista Youth Organization, as another case in point, had only 1,500 members at the commencement of the CNA. During the crusade, these militants served as heads of brigades; they were responsible for discipline and conduct, as well as the political education of the *brigadistas.* (Not infrequently they also served as political mentors of the teacher supervisors.)[60] By the end of the crusade, membership in the JS-19 J had mushroomed to over 20,000 and as of 1984 to approximately 40,000 militants. In 1983, 53 percent of the Sandinista Youth militants participated in defense activities, and more than 20,000 volunteered to be members of production brigades for the 1983–84 harvest.[61]

The linkage between participation in the CNA, membership in Sandinista political organizations, and involvement in national revolutionary tasks is seen in the overlapping roles played by the delegates to the Sandinista Youth Organization's national youth assembly in Managua, December 19–21, 1981. Of the 560 delegates in attendance, 547 were militants of the Sandinista National Liberation Front (FSLN), 467 had been production *brigadistas,* 322 were veteran guerrilla fighters from the struggle to overthrow Somoza, and 496 had been literacy teachers in the CNA.[62]

The crusade also extended these mass organizations into regions that had a paucity of social services and little experience in unionization or political interest articulation. On the Atlantic Coast, for example, the CNA is credited with greatly strengthening the National Educators' Association. And according to Ministry of Education personnel in Puerto Cabezas, the literacy workers also helped organize the Association of Rural Workers.

Integrating the Atlantic Coast

The campaign in indigenous languages in 1980–81 signaled the intentions of the national government to integrate the Atlantic Coast with the rest of the country while respecting its cultures. Philippe Bourgois describes the campaign's intended outcomes in this way: "By emphasizing . . . what appears superficially to contradict national unity—the distinctive identities of the ethnic minorities—a greater trust and sympathy for the government is actually promoted."[63] In keeping with this thrust the government made special efforts to train indigenous instructional personnel (over three-fourths of the literacy teachers in the campaign came from the region) and to revise the literacy materials from the CNA to reflect (in the photographs, drawings, and content) the people, terrain, economy, and culture of the Atlantic Coast.

Among the integrative outcomes of the literacy campaigns on the East Coast are a greater familiarity with written Spanish on the part of the indigenous population, an awareness of national symbols and figures like Sandino, and a sharing in the folk culture (music, dance, poetry, legends) of the Pacific Coast peoples. Furthermore, the campaigns brought with them access to other important services, particularly in the area of health: thousands were furnished with eyeglasses, inoculated, and referred to health centers.

Serious problems also have beset the literacy campaigns and the follow-up programs in adult education. Steadman Fagoth Mueller, a leader of the Miskito people and the indigenous association MISURASATA (Miskitu, Sumu, Rama, Sandinistas "All Together") used the campaign to help reach and organize Miskitos to demand a degree of autonomy for Atlantic Coast inhabitants that was considered by the Sandinista government to be prejudicial to national unity. In February 1981, when Fagoth was detained by the Sandinista government, a great number of Miskito Indians pulled out of the language campaign, and when Fagoth subsequently escaped to Honduras in May 1981, thousands went with him.

Since late 1981, large tracts of the Atlantic Coast region have comprised a war zone; this is particularly true of the area bordering Honduras, where many Miskito villages were located. There have been innumerable incursions by counterrevolutionaries (*contras*), many of them Miskito Indians under the leadership of Fagoth, and a smaller number under the leadership of Brooklyn Rivera with his base in Costa Rica. By early 1982, approximately 8,500 Miskito Indians were forcibly removed to resettlement camps some 35 miles inland from where they had been; the relocation was undertaken by the Sandinista government to remove a sanctuary and supply base for counterrevolutionary activity as well as to protect the lives and safety of the inhabitants in what had been a "free fire zone."

Needless to say, educational activities and other national social services have been disrupted by the conflict. On the other hand, a number of past mistakes by the Sandinista government, including cultural insensitivity in the selection of political and civic functionaries for different public agencies, are now being rectified. Subsequent chapters will note efforts of the national government to implement bilingual education at the primary education level, establish needed technical training and adult education programs, recruit leaders respected by indigenous communities for important posts in the fields of education and culture, and build upon existing indigenous organizations for development efforts. The Declaration of Principles of the Sandinista Revolution on the Atlantic Coast states the intention of the national government to involve the different ethnic populations in determining public policy for the region. The declaration reads, "The Sandinista Popular Revolution will support and guarantee the participation of the communities of the Atlantic Coast in the resolution of all the social, economic, and political problems which affect not only them, but the entire nation. . . . All the different forms which communities develop to organize themselves will be supported, thus assuring a true representation of the population in the different social, political, and economic decisions that are made regarding the Atlantic Coast."[64]

The integration of the Atlantic Coast remains problematic. The region still contains separatist and hostile elements and many more who are taking a cautious wait-and-see approach; and even among the pro-government supporters who worked actively in the literacy campaign, there is a strong sense of regionalism and a desire for more resources to be channeled to the coast. While the CNA and follow-up educational activities stimulated greater national awareness on the part of the people and strengthened several mass organizations national in scope, the progressive integration of the region will depend, more fundamentally, on major improvements in transportation and communication systems, on the availability of capital for economic development, and the working out of modus operandi by which the natural resources of the Atlantic Coast can be jointly exploited by indigenous communities and the national government to the satisfaction of both sides.[65] This modus operandi, in turn, will have to be part of an overall negotiated settlement in which the autonomy of the indigenous populations will be congruent with the Sandinista goals of a unified nation in which all segments can participate and benefit.

THE LITERACY CRUSADE AS A MODEL OF EDUCATIONAL AND SOCIAL CHANGE

The CNA served as a model of voluntary collective effort to resolve pressing social needs. This model has been applied to subsequent efforts in nonformal education and to other areas such as health. For example, in October 1981 over 70,000 trained volunteers were mobilized for a three-day period to distribute antimalarial pills to approximately 75 percent of the Nicaraguan population.

This mobilization was based on the multiplier model of training first demonstrated in the literacy campaign. The model takes the form of a pyramid of trainers. In the case of the CNA, 80 trainers (half teachers and half university students) were first prepared in a 15-day course followed by one month of field experience. These 80 then trained approximately 600. The multiplier effect then proceeded in this fashion: the 560 trained more than 11,000 (mostly teachers) who trained over 100,000 literacy workers. The process took approximately three months. Thus, large numbers of people can be prepared in a brief period.

The national literacy crusade further demonstrated the philosophy of the Sandinista regime that when the people want a basic service they can provide it to themselves through their communal efforts. The role of the government is to assist with mobilizing the population and providing necessary material support, training, and technical advice. This approach breaks with the elitism of a model based on professionals monopolizing knowledge and exclusively controlling delivery of services in essential areas such as education and health.

The Ecuadoran educator Rosa María Torres succinctly summarizes the new model of education: "The Crusade had been, in effect, the great laboratory where they tested the ingredients of a new model of education congruent with the historical project of the Revolution, in which the people are the principal actors and objects of this project.[66] For people to view themselves as the principal actors in a process of national reconstruction, they must undergo a change of mentality and political consciousness. As Torres goes on to note, the transformation of consciousness, as exemplified by the CNA, "is not an individual act but a basic social process of formation of collective consciousness . . . and the formation of that new collective consciousness cannot be accomplished at the margin of concrete social practice, but in the process of transforming reality."[67]

QUESTIONS AND CONCLUSIONS

What impact did the literacy campaign have on the political culture of Nicaragua, on the stated goal of the "humanistic transformation of Nicaraguan society"?[68] Five years after the termination of the crusade, it is possible to point to positive outcomes. The CNA played a critical role in helping to overcome the inequities between countryside and city, males and females, the Atlantic and Pacific Coasts. It contributed to the mobilization and induction of previously marginal populations—peasantry and women, the youth and the aged—into new roles related to national reconstruction. The crusade also played an important role in strengthening mass organizations—notably the Sandinista Youth (JS-19 J), the National Educators' Association (ANDEN), and the Nicaraguan Women's Association (AMNLAE).

Another important outcome is the notion that people are not only recipients of culture, but creators of culture.[69] In the land of Rubén Darío, recently literate peasants are writing poetry, and scores of poetry workshops have been established in factories, union headquarters, army bases, and farming cooperative centers.[70] At the same time, the mass consumption of Nicaraguan and Latin American classics is another facet of the remarkable cultural changes occurring in the country. The public demand for inexpensive literature, and printed material in general, has increased dramatically over the past five years. Prior to the CNA, there was no national publishing industry in Nicaragua. The literacy campaign, among other milestone events, marked the beginnings of that industry, in that the CNA produced and distributed over one million different texts and pamphlets; the follow-up adult education program was to place even greater demands on the national publishing capacity.

Finally, the CNA established a new model of social change based on substantial devolution of decision-making powers to the grass-roots level. It demonstrated that communities through their own effort, and in conjunction with the government, can provide basic social services. According to Torres, the crusade initiated the process of administrative decentralization of the country,[71] whereby the country is divided into nine regions and substantial authority is delegated to local governmental entities and mass organizations.

The limitations of the campaign must also be noted: male-female relations do not change that easily, the integration of the Atlantic Coast involves a substantial number of obstacles, and the initial good will and support for the regime engendered by the CNA—widely regarded as perhaps the single most outstanding achievement of the revolution—is also contingent upon government initiatives in other areas. Also problematic is the level of literacy skills attained by people in such a brief period. Further, how reasonable is it to expect significant changes in individual life circumstances or community living standards as a result of enhanced literacy skills?

In many respects, the literacy campaign never ended. For even before the mid-August deadline approached for terminating the activities of the *brigadistas* in the countryside, plans were already under way to select community leaders who would assume the role of instructors in the follow-up adult education programs. The process of mass education was merely beginning. The continuation of this story is the focus of Chapter 3.

NOTES

1. Nicaraguan Ministry of Education, "The Great National Literacy Campaign: Heroes and Martyrs for the Creation of Nicaragua." mimeographed report, translated and edited by the National Network in Solidarity with the Nicaraguan People (Managua, Nicaraguan Ministry of Education, January 1980), p. 1.

2. Comments made by Richard Fagen to the panel on "The Nicaraguan Revolution: A New Model?" (9th National Meeting of the Latin American Studies Association, Bloomington, Indiana, October 18, 1980).

3. For a detailed study of the role of the National Guard in maintaining the Somoza family in power for a period of four decades, see Richard Millett, *Guardians of the Dynasty* (New York: Orbis, 1977).

4. Arthur Gillette, *Cuba's Educational Revolution,* (London: Fabian Society, 1972), p. 20. Gillette actually distinguishes between education *for* communism and education *in* communism.

5. Interview with Rev. Fernando Cardenal, at the national headquarters of the Sandinista Defense Committees (CDS), Managua, Nicaragua, June 7, 1984.

Father Cardenal was national coordinator of the Literacy Crusade. After the CNA, he became vice-coordinator for the Sandinista Youth (JS–19 J). At the time of the interview, he was vice-coordinator of the Sandinista Defense Committees. In July 1984, he became Minister of Education.

6. For a statement of the CNA as a political priority of the Sandinista government, see Guillermo Rothschuh Tablada and Carlos Tamez, *La Cruzada Nacional de Alfabetización de Nicaragua: Su Organización y Estrategias de Participación y Mobilización* (Paris: UNESCO, 1983), p. 56.

7. The People's Literacy Teachers (Los Alfabetizadores Populares—AP) consisted of two types: over 20,000 "Urban Literacy Guerrillas," who taught in the urban neighborhoods, and some 3,000 worker-teachers who taught in the factories and comprised the "Workers' Literacy Militias."

8. For further discussion on the recruitment of literacy teachers, see Jan L. Flora, John McFadden, and Ruth Warner, "The Growth of Class Struggle: The Impact of the Nicaraguan Literacy Crusade on the Political Consciousness of Young Literacy Workers," *Latin American Perspectives* 36 (Winter 1983): 53–55.

9. Detailed description of logistical problems posed by the CNA is found in Chapter 5 of Rothschuh Tablada and Tamez, *Cruzada Nacional.*

10. See Charles L. Stansifer, "The Nicaraguan National Literacy Crusade," American University Field Staff Reports, South America, No. 6, p. 5.

11. Instruction in mathematical concepts using the primer *Calculo y Reactivación: Una Sola Operación* was of secondary importance and was not undertaken until the student had completed lesson seven of the literacy primer and had achieved basic literacy skills. See Miller, *National Literacy Crusade,* p. 101.

12. It is interesting to note that the photograph used in lesson 23 of the literacy primer to indicate solidarity with liberation struggles in other countries is of the prime minister of Vietnam and two members of the government junta, Alfonso Robelo and Violeta Chamorro, who left the government in the spring of 1980, and have since become opponents of the Sandinista regime. The revised 1984 literacy primer which is being used in the ongoing program of adult education, needless to say, does not have this photograph.

13. Hirshon, *Also Teach Them,* p. 104.

14. Freire, "Adult Literacy Process"; and Freire, *Pedagogy of the Oppressed.*

15. A parallel situation existed in Cuba. See the discussion of Jonathan Kozol. "A New Look at the Literacy Campaign in Cuba," *Harvard Educational Review* 48 (Summer 1978): 341–77, especially 354.

16. Paulo Freire visited Nicaragua for a nine-day period prior to the commencement of the CNA. After consulting with the team of educators designing the campaign, he announced his enthusiastic support for both its content and pedagogy.

17. See, for example, the discussion of Kozol, "Literacy Campaign in Cuba," p. 364.

18. For further discussion along these lines, see Robert F. Arnove and Jairo Arboleda, "Literacy: Power or Mystification?" *Literacy Discussion* 4 (December 1973): 389–414.

19. See, for example, Martin Carnoy, *Education as Cultural Imperialism* (New York: McKay, 1974), esp. Chap. 1.

20. Eighty percent of the children in rural areas were not in school, and 21 percent of the illiterates in the country were accounted for by youths in the age group 10–14. Under 25 percent of the appropriate age group (13–18) were enrolled in secondary school, while according to the *Encyclopedia of the Third World* (ed.) George Thomas Kurian (New York: Facts on File, 1978), 2: 1065, 5.38 per 1,000 (about 8 percent) of the appropriate age group were enrolled in universities. Nicaragua ranked 86th in the world in adjusted school enrollment for primary and secondary education, but 61st in per capita university enrollment in 1976. For further discussion of educational neglect, see Chapter 1.

21. Hirshon, *Also Teach Them,* p. 105.

22. For further discussion, see Philippe Bourgois, "Class, Ethnicity and the State among the Miskito Amerindians of Northeastern Nicaragua," *Latin American Perspectives* 29 (Spring 1981): 22–39; also his, "Nicaragua's Ethnic Minorities in the Revolution," *Monthly Review* 37 (January 1985): 22–39; and Philip A. Dennis, "The Costeños and the Revolution in Nicaragua," *Journal of Interamerican Studies and World Affairs* 23 (August 1981): 271–96.

23. According to the Center for Information and Documentation of the Atlantic Coast (INICCA), 63 percent of the costeños are Spanish-speaking Latinos; 24 percent Miskito-speaking; 10 percent English-speaking; 2.5 percent Sumospeaking; .47 percent Garifundi-speaking, and .24 percent Rama-speaking. For further discussion, see National Network in Solidarity with the Nicaraguan People, "Atlantic Coast: Miskitu Crisis and Counterrevolution," *Nicaragua* (May-June 1982), pp. 4–5, reprinted in *The Nicaragua Reader,* ed. Peter Rosset and John Vandermeer (New York: Grove Press, 1982), p. 83.

24. For discussion of the census taken to ascertain the level of illiteracy in the country, see Fernando Cardenal, S.J. and Valerie Miller, "Nicaragua 1980: The Battle of the ABCs," *Harvard Educational Review,* 51 (February 1981): 13–14.

25. Illiteracy was relatively low among the English-speaking inhabitants, who tend to be fundamentalist Protestants placing great emphasis on reading the Bible.

26. According to Bulletin no. 13 of La Cruzada en Marcha (Managua: CNA/Ministry of Education, July 1980), p. 7, *brigadistas* helped build 2,862 latrines, 75 wells, 96 schools, 34 roads, 50 bridges, 37 health centers, and had participated in the planting and harvesting of thousands of acres of various fruits and vegetables.

27. For further details, see H.S. Bhola, *Campaigning for Literacy* (Paris: UNESCO, 1982), pp. 161–85.

28. Jonathan Kozol, however, in his article "Literacy Campaign in Cuba," p. 360, estimates that by early 1961 the illiteracy rate was less than 20 percent due to experimental programs conducted during 1959 and 1960. Still, as he points out no other Latin American country had reduced its illiteracy rate to as low as 8 percent of its population, and the Latin American median illiteracy in 1960 was 32.5 percent.

29. See, for example, Robert Leiken, "Nicaragua's Untold Story," *New Republic,* October 8, 1984: 19.

30. See DEI, *Nicaragua Triunfa en la Alfabetización,* ed. Hugo Assmann (Managua: Ministry of Education, and San José, Costa Rica: Departamento Ecuménico de Investigaciones, 1981), p. 194.

31. Hirshon, *And Teach Them to Read,* p. 75.

32. Interview with Carlos Carrión, at the headquarters of the Sandinista Youth (JS-19 J) Managua, June 21, 1984. Carrión is national director of the organization.

33. Valerie Miller, "The Nicaraguan Literacy Crusade," in Walker (ed.), *Nicaragua in Revolution,* 244.

34. Beverly Treumann, "Nicaragua's Second Revolution," *Christianity and Crisis* 41 (November 2, 1981), pp. 297–98.

35. Carlos Tünnermann Bernheim, "One Year Later," in *Nicaragua for the Eradication of Illiteracy,* ed. Jan Kaspar (Paris: International Union of Students and UNESCO, n.d.).

36. Treumann, "Nicaragua's Second Revolution," pp. 297–98.

37. Interview of June 21, 1984, see n. 32.

38. FSLN, *Participatory Democracy in Nicaragua* (Managua: FSLN, 1984), pp. 58–59. The book is available in English or Spanish at the International Press Center at the Hotel Intercontinental.

39. Flora et al., "Impact of Literacy Crusade," pp. 49–51.

40. Ibid., pp. 56–7.

41. Ibid., p. 59.

42. Ibid., p. 53.

43. Treumann, "Nicaragua's Second Revolution," p. 299.

44. Hirshon, *And Teach Them to Read,* p. 211.

45. Ibid., p. 62.

46. Interview with Pablo Centeno-Gómez, at his home in Managua, June 2, 1984.

47. Anita Mikkonen, "The Literacy Crusade and the Children," in Kaspar (ed.) *Eradication of Illiteracy.*

48. Cardenal and Miller, "Nicaragua 1980," p. 12.

49. Ibid., p. 25.

50. Warren Hoge, "Women Win New Role in Nicaragua," *Austin American Statesman,* January 15, 1981, p. E–4.

51. Interview with Fernando Cardenal, see n. 5.

52. For further details, see Asociación de Mujeres Nicaragüenses "Luisa Amanda Espinoza" (AMNLAE), "Women's Participation in the New Nicaragua," in *Contemporary Marxism* No. 8, special issue entitled, "Nicaragua under Siege" (Spring 1984): 122–28, esp. 126–27.

53. Interview with Magda Enríquez, at national headquarters of AMNLAE, Managua, May 25, 1984.

54. The ban applies, for example, to mass media advertising; see Hoge, "Women Win New Role."

55. AMNLAE, "Women's Participation," pp. 126–27.

56. Ibid., p. 127.

57. Treumann, "Nicaragua's Second Revolution," p. 295.

58. Interview with Edgardo García, secretary general, at the national headquarters of the Rural Workers' Association, Managua, May 22, 1984.

59. Interview with Nubia Pavallaccini at the national headquarters of the National Educators' Association, Managua, June 15, 1984.

60. See, for example, the descriptions of the role played by the brigade leader in Hirshon, *And Teach Them to Read.*

61. Interview with Carlos Carrión, see n. 32.

62. Onofre Guevara L., "La JS 19: Una Posición Ganada en la Lucha," *Barricada,* December 22, 1981: 3.

63. Bourgois, "Miskito Amerindians," p. 37.

64. Nicaraguan Institute for the Atlantic Coast (INNICA), Declaration of the Principles of the Sandinista Revolution on the Atlantic Coast," *Bulletin* 7 (October 1981).

65. William Ramírez, "El Problema Indígena y la Amenaza Imperialista en Nicaragua," in the magazine section *Vergara, Barricada,* January 6, 1982: 13–14.

66. Rosa María Torres, *De Alfabetizando a Maestro Popular: La Post-Alfabetización en Nicaragua* (Managua: Instituto de Investigaciones Económicas y Sociales, 1983), p. 10. My translation from Spanish.

67. Ibid.

68. Carlos Tünnermann Bernheim, in *Primer Congreso Nacional de Educación Popular de Adultos* (Managua: Ministry of Education, June 6–7, 1981), p. 21.

69. "Pluralism and Popular Power: An Interview with Sergio Ramírez Mercado," in *Contemporary Marxism,* "Nicaragua under Siege," p. 172.

70. See Stansifer, "Nicaraguan Literacy Crusade," p. 49.

71. Torres, *Post-Alfabetización,* p. 10.

3
Popular Education

The transformation of a people is based on the transformation of education at all levels.[1]

During the literacy crusade, it was frequently said by the Sandinista leadership that "Nicaragua was converted into one big school." The notion of society and the revolutionary context as educator, a common theme in Cuba after 1959, is also typical of Nicaragua in the post-1979 period. During the armed struggle to overthrow the Somoza regime, thousands of young and old people learned needed skills, changed perceptions, and gained new identities. Similarly, during and after the literacy crusade, tens of thousands were mobilized into new roles as teachers and learners.

Despite the impressive gains wrought by the literacy crusade, the level of skills acquired during the campaign was minimal. Increasingly higher levels of language and computational skills, as well as technical and vocational knowledge, were required to make improvements in communities, raise living standards, and generate greater economic abundance. Organizational skills were required to participate in and manage the mass organizations, such as ATC, CDS, and AMNLAE, which have become key agencies for implementation of public policy in the areas of health, defense, social welfare, and education.

The demands for a better educated citizenry are being generated by the transformations taking place in the society. By the end of 1984, the government's land reform program, for example, had distributed over 2 million acres to some 50,000 families (over 200,000 people). In the initial phase of land reform, a majority of the land was distributed to cooperatives.[2] Over 75,000 farmers have joined the newly created National Union of Farmers and Cattle Ranchers (UNAG) in some 3,057 cooperatives.[3]

With land reform, there also has been a substantial increase in credit for small and medium-size farmers and cooperatives: for example, between 1979 and 1982, 1.62 billion *cordobas* of credit were distributed to farmers, as compared with 112 million *cordobas* of credit in 1977. As one *campesino* noted to a delegation of North American scholars visiting the country to observe the November 1984 elections, "Now I can go to a bank myself; I can talk to a government official."[4] In addition to demands created by these changes in rural life, rural workers needed to be informed about their rights gained under new policies concerning minimum wages and occupational health and safety. Further, as a number of owners sought to disinvest and send capital overseas, workers needed to be informed about these attempts to decapitalize the large farms and the rural enterprises for which they worked, and what they could do about the situation.[5]

Women, too, had new needs for education and training. As noted in the previous chapter, the revolution opened new roles to women. For example, women account for 40 percent of the membership in UNAG cooperatives. They occupy important positions in defense activities and government, particularly at the regional level. As the former head of the education unit of AMNLAE noted, women need to know how to conduct a meeting, develop a work plan, fill out an application for a bank loan, and assume administrative positions in a variety of state agencies and mass organizations.[6]

If the revolutionary context has opened up multiple educational opportunities for previously disadvantaged populations, it also has been characterized by a number of constraints and problems. Programs to achieve the goals of rapid economic growth and greater social justice have had to be implemented within the bounds of a beseiged, underdeveloped country.

Within this context, the challenge to the government has been how to extend the benefits of education, as well as health, housing, and other basic social services, to the most disadvantaged sectors of the society. As Chapter 2 noted, the CNA had offered a model of what could be done to provide literacy to the majority of people even in the most remote regions of the country. The elements of this model are the following: 1) a *campaign* or a *mobilization* of large numbers of people around a theme—for example, the eradication of illiteracy or elimination of malaria and polio; 2) the use of *multiplier chains,* progressively larger numbers of people training others; 3) the *empowering* of *nonprofessionals* with the necessary knowledge and skills to perform tasks previously monopolized by professionals; 4) the use of *mass organizations* as mechanisms of implementation—the role of the state being to provide guidelines, funding, and initial training; 5) the creative use of symbols and indigenous art forms as well as the mass media to rouse people and convey new messages to formerly alienated populations; 6) the attempt to fuse pedagogy and content, political socialization and technical training to raise consciousness, impart different values, and form a more active and inquiring Nicaraguan person.

Elements of this model are found in the educational activities that have been undertaken by the mass organizations in the post-1979 period to train their own staffs, improve the organizational and technical skills of their members, and transform the political culture of the country. The one program and form of mass organization which perhaps best exemplifies the new model of "popular education," in the sense that it derives from and serves the common person, is *Educación Popular Básica* (EPB). The remainder of this chapter briefly describes the history of adult education programs in Nicaragua prior to 1979, and the working of EPB and the nonformal education activities of the mass organizations that complement EPB. The strengths and limitations of both adult and nonformal education will be analyzed.

ADULT EDUCATION DURING
THE SOMOZA PERIOD

Prior to the establishment of a Vice-Ministry of Adult Education (VIMEDA) in October 1980, adult education had been principally the responsibility of the private sector. Within the Ministry of Education, adult education was a department of the Division of Primary Education. Macías Gómez, who conducted a review of the field of adult education in the mid-1970s, concluded that there was no system of adult education, in the sense of a set of interrelated agencies and activities. Instead, he found a group of isolated and unrelated institutions applying distinctive educational concepts and methods.[7] According to the researcher, the most successful adult education programs were found in the nongovernmental sector, where the subject was treated with "greater civic seriousness and professionalism."[8] Of the 20 private sector institutions included in the survey, 50 percent were of a religious nature and 90 percent of the programs received help from foreign sources, with government financing accounting for only 20 percent of revenues.[9]

The pronouncements of the Somoza administration about the goals of adult education were remarkably similar in some respects to those of the Sandinistas. For example, Ministry of Education publications of the Somoza era discuss the active incorporation of adults into community life, the skilled and critical participation of adults in the various aspects of national reconstruction, and the need for a scientific explanation of natural phenomena and society.[10] This rhetoric, however, was matched by neither the will nor the resources to implement stated goals. The utterances and policies of the deposed Somoza regime must be seen within a context of dependence and underdevelopment. Adult education and literacy programs served largely promotional and cooptive purposes, and in the case of Plan Waslala of 1977–79, intelligence gathering and national security ends. As Barndt notes, the 108 "literacy teachers" who were appointed to the region of Waslala in the North of Nicaragua as part of a counterinsurgency strategy were in fact "security agents who identified FSLN sympathizers, leading to some of the most brutal peasant massacres. . . ."[11]

Moreover, the perspectives that undergirded adult education programs during the final years of the Somoza regime were those of "human capital theory," "structural-functionalism," and "modernization," in which the workforce is expected to uncritically adapt to technological change and technological change per se comprises development.[12] This ideological underpinning differs considerably from the class analysis of the FSLN and its definition of development in relation to national independence and social justice. Central Questions deriving from the perspective employed by the Sandinistas are who controls technology, for what purposes, and who are the beneficiaries of greater abundance? In the realm of education, the organization, content, form, and workings of the new system of adult and nonformal (popular) education illuminate the basic differences between the ideological orientations and development perspectives of the pre- and post-1979 political regimes.

CHARACTERISTICS OF *EDUCACION POPULAR BASICA*—EPB

EPB comprises the system of adult education that succeeded the National Literacy Crusade (March 23–August 23, 1980) and the sustainment program (August 1980–February 1981) to maintain the skills of those who had participated in the CNA. The *sostenimiento* program also was established to continue the education of those who had not achieved literacy during the campaign. The organizational form that EPB took was that of educational collectives (*Colectivos de Educación Popular*—CEPs). EPB began in March 1980 under the auspices of the newly created Vice-Ministry of Adult Education.

EPB relies principally on the Sandinista mass organizations and nonprofessionals as the agencies of continuing education. Many of the teacher-animators or popular educators are graduates of the literacy campaign. Four percent of the *maestros populares* in 1983, according to Torres, had become literate during the literacy campaign, 16 percent were studying the first level of adult education, and 32 percent had only completed a few years of primary school education.[13] There is also in the EPB reliance on the youth of the country to shoulder much of the responsibility for instruction. The case described by the former Vice-Minister of Adult Education, Francisco Lacayo, of a 12-year-old youth with only two years of schooling who was a popular teacher (*coordinador*) of 13 students and a supervisor (*promotor*) of five CEPs may be somewhat unusual.[14] But during the first four years of EPB, approximately 10 percent of the popular educators were between 10 and 14 years old, and over one-third were between 15 and 19. Another 25 percent were in the age group 20 to 24, and only about 30 percent of all coordinators were 25 years or older.

This volunteer and youthful teaching force, using inexpensive print material and a variety of classroom settings, by mid-1984 had enabled adult education to reach approximately 195,000 Nicaraguans in some 17,000 educational collectives. The CEPs, as with the 60,000 literacy units (UAS) during the literacy crusade, are located in schools, churches, public buildings, and homes. The CEPs meet five times a week, usually at night, two hours per day. On Saturdays, the popular teachers attend workshops conducted by *promotores* to upgrade their skills.

In effect, EPB comprises an adult-centered, community-based parallel education system to the formal school system. It offers an introductory course in literacy for those who were not reached during the CNA or who did not achieve literacy from March to August 1980. As of 1984, EPB consisted of six levels (semesters) of instruction. The curriculum for the first four levels concentrates on language arts and mathematics, with other subjects integrated into the respective language and mathematics texts *Nuestra Trinchera* (Our Trench) and *En Marcha* (On the March). Separate texts exist at the fifth and sixth levels for the areas of social and natural sciences. Students progress through EPB by passing a series of partial and final examinations.

By the end of 1984, VIMEDA had decided to extend the program of Basic Popular Education through nine levels. In part, this decision was motivated by the lack of formal equivalence of different levels of EPB with those of the regular school system. For example, completion of the sixth level of EPB does not confer on graduates the equivalent of a primary school diploma. Further, there was the question of the desirability and appropriateness of EPB graduates attending conventional primary and secondary education programs. Instead, the last three cycles of EPB (seven through nine) are to concentrate on teaching vocational skills. Another concern was that EPB would be used by many of its younger students as a stepping stone to the formal education ladder rather than as an alternative form of preparation for entry into the work force as skilled or semi-skilled workers.

One of the interesting features of EPB is that during the first four years of its existence, approximately one-fifth of all students have been under 15 years of age and another one-fourth to one-fifth have been between 15 and 19 years old. The reasons for this situation are the poverty of the country and the need for children and youth to work to help sustain their families and to assist with household chores during the day. Without EPB, many youths would not be able to attend any form of systematic education. In many CEPs it is not uncommon to find children learning along with adults; and in some cases, several generations of the same family work together by day and study side-by-side at night.

In urban locations, where larger schools are found, it is possible to group students by age and provide separate instruction. The younger popular educators frequently teach the youngest pupils. But in rural areas, where 80 percent of the CEPs are found, there is little possibility of sorting students out by age or level of instruction. Most CEPs are therefore "mixed" or heterogeneous.

Instructional guidelines all stress that the learning is to actively engage students in the observation, interpretation and analysis of their life circumstances. Thought is then expected to lead to action. The natural sciences text, for example, states, "We can only say we have learned something when we are capable of applying [knowledge] to transform little by little our reality." To this end, lesson plans of the various texts frequently call upon students to write letters, send telegrams, talk to friends, and put into practice ideas that they have read about or discussed in the CEPs. A number of the CEPs use sociodramas or role playing, small group discussion, development of class montages of newspaper and magazine clippings to illustrate and explore social issues. Once a week, the FSLN newspaper, *Barricada,* publishes a page that contains a theme discussed in simple language and printed in large type so that it can be used as part of ongoing adult education activities. Twice daily (5:30–6:00), the program *Puño en Alto*[15] is broadcast over all radio stations providing suggestions for instructional activities and featuring the accomplishments of CEPs from different regions of the country.

As in other areas of national life, artistic expression is encouraged. Adults who were illiterate before the CNA are writing poetry in CEPs. Regardless of the level of sophistication, it is a moving experience to encounter the poems written by the students of EPB. The following poem was written by a mother of four who was studying at the third level at a CEP in the mountain town of Jinotega:

Poema a Germán Pomares
Germán Pomares Ordoñes
Germán pensaban que
con matarte la lucha había
terminado. Pero no la
lucha se siguió por toda
Nicaragua. Con la esperansa

de algun día nuestra causa
se ha cumplido gracia a los
que lucharon con las armas
en la mano. Lo cual ahora
estamos en una patría libre
Germán, tu deseo se ha cumplido.
Patría libre o morir.

María de Rosario Zeledon
Age 32

Poem to Germán Pomares
Germán Pomares Ordoñes
Germán they thought that
by killing you the struggle would
end. But no the
struggle continues throughout all
of Nicaragua. With the hope
that some day our cause
will have been achieved thanks to
those who struggle with arms
in hand. Thus today
we live in a free country.
Germán, your wish has been realized.
A free country or death.

Artistic standards aside, the poem is indicative of the political imagery that suffuses much artistic expression. A lot of poetry concerns not only past "heroes and martyrs of the Revolution," but the images of everyday struggle—and triumph—in a country endeavoring to forge a new destiny.

The primers, for the most part, reflect not only the pedagogical notions of praxis (action guided by thought) but the political priorities and programs of the FSLN. Their content clearly is intended to safeguard and advance the Sandinista revolution as well as transform the political culture of the country. From the cover page on, the text and illustrations systematically echo the national priorities of increased production, defense, and national sovereignty. While the general readers tend to be explicitly political in content, this is much less the case with the mathematics and natural science texts. These texts, generally, are less overtly doctrinaire or partisan, although they repeatedly discuss content in relation to the activities of cooperatives, agrarian reform, meeting production quotas, and the new roles of peasants, women, and inhabitants of the Atlantic Coast in post-Somoza Nicaragua. Below are some examples from different EPB texts.

In the cooperative of Silvio Mayorga in Pancasán, 5,814 cans of coffee were harvested. Of this amount, 3,484 were sold. The remainder was left for consumption. How many cans [each can = apx. 2.5 gallons] of coffee remained in the cooperative?

(third level mathematics, 1st partial test)

The other project in Muy-Muy-Matigua is long range. By means of an investment of 580 million *cordobas,* this project is trying to achieve in a period of 10 years an additional annual production of 13.2 million gallons [of milk].

(A series of mathematical exercises are then based on the above information—sixth level mathematics)

Caminemos (Let's Go Together), the EPB text used for people involved in harvests and defense mobilizations offers a number of instances of explicit political socialization. A unit describing and illustrating with photographs the activities of Sandinista militias and frontier guards has a glossary of words including blackmail, sovereignty, annihilate, repel, and detect. The definition of blackmail, for example, reads: "Crimes that consist of obtaining money or advantage under different types of threat." Example: "*Imperialism blackmails us when it offers us loans under conditions that are prejudicial to us*" [emphasis in text].

A subsequent section of *Caminemos* (pp. 41–48) confronts the rumors being circulated by the counterrevolutionaries that the heavy rains and flooding that afflicted the country in 1982 were signs of God's displeasure with the Sandinista government. A series of cartoon figures explain the causes of rain, the actual damage resulting from the flooding, the relief aid provided by friendly nations, and recommendations for the students to write a letter to a friend or family member describing what they know about the natural calamity. In addition, a set of mathematical exercises concerns seven families that are in a refugee camp because of the rains.

Generally, the mathematical and natural science lessons and examinations require problem-solving skills and higher-order cognitive processes involving interpretation and generalization. A fifth level science test, for example, asks students to name the types of soils according to their mineral properties and what can be done to control soil erosion.

On the other hand, examinations in the social studies and reading areas of popular education tend to require pat answers. The first test of language usage in the introductory levels of EPB asks the students to write the name of Sandino as well as to paint it on walls and to shout the slogan, "Sandino Yesterday, Today, and Forever." The test goes on to ask, "What does the slogan 'Sandino Yesterday, Today, and Forever' signify for us?"

and "Why do we say that Sandino did not die on February 21?" Also: "How do we continue on a daily basis the struggle of Sandino?" Students are then asked to write a sentence with each of the following words: Sandino, enemy, patriot, education. While these lower-order questions and tasks may be attributed to the fact that the student population is only at the introductory level of literacy, a fifth level social science test also fails to offer any questions that elicit critical thought. The first test in this subject simply asks students to select from among three alternatives the name of indigenous markets, to identify which group exercised power in indigenous society, to fill in a blank as to which class worked with the *criollos,* to name the tax that the Spanish crown imposed on indigenous peoples, and to identify the type of government characteristic of the indigenous population. A last question asks the ways in which imperialism is violating the country.

The above examples of traditional pedagogy based on rote memorization and pat responses is representative of one set of problems associated with popular education. The following sections describes in greater detail the programs of providing basic adult education in an underdeveloped country that lacks adequate resources and is also facing internal and external aggression. These problems include poorly prepared instructors, high burnout and dropout rates of both students and teachers, the lack of articulation of popular education with the formal education system and vocational training, and the danger of political education that simply indoctrinates rather than stimulates people to be critically conscious political participants in the processes of social change.

PROBLEMS AND CONTRADICTIONS OF EPB

Viewed in relation to its own stated goals and philosophy, EPB manifests a number of significant shortcomings. More seriously, some of the very aims and emphases of the program contradict one another. While it is possible that tension between different components of the program may lead to creative resolution of existing problems, it is also probable that they could effectively limit the positive outcomes of adult education efforts.

Poverty and Aggression

A number of the problems derive, as noted earlier, from the poverty of the country. The following description in the 1982 October/November issue of *Nicaragua* is fairly typical of the challenges facing EPB:

Rural areas often lack adequate facilities for CEPs. 70 percent of the collectives in Rivas lack sufficient seating, writing surfaces or blackboards. Three of the seven areas in Estelí are without electricity and many CEPs have not been able to meet because new wicks for Coleman lanterns are not available. Some areas are only reachable by boat and the gasoline supply is often insufficient for supervisors to visit classes and provide materials. It is common for supervisors and popular educators to travel from two to five hours on foot to attend a workshop or meeting.

Special problems exist in agricultural communities. From September to March 1981, 50 percent of the *campesinos* with no land or with small holdings dropped out of the program to migrate north for the harvests.[16]

The aggression directed against the Sandinista regime by the U.S.-backed counterrevolutionaries is another source of problems. As of May 1984, 158 teachers had either died in combat or had been assassinated while teaching; of this number 135 were popular educators in EPB. Educators and health workers comprise special targets of *contra* attacks as they are symbols of the social changes occurring in the country. In addition, in 1984, 840 CEPs were not functioning as the result of direct sabotage or because of the danger to students attending evening classes in areas with intensive counterrevolutionary activity. Adult education activities have had to be largely suspended in the border area with Honduras and in large tracts of the northeastern region. Mobilization of CEP participants for defense activities or to assist with production brigades harvesting various export crops also has negatively affected adult education activities.

Preparation and Sophistication of Teachers

What has been viewed as a strength of popular education efforts in Nicaragua—thousands of minimally schooled volunteers serving as teachers—may also be a serious shortcoming. As the above-cited article in *Nicaragua* notes, "70 percent of the popular educators have not yet finished sixth grade—many, in fact, are only one step ahead of their student neighbors."[17] Other writers, however, view the large-scale use of these community volunteers as a unique strength of EPB. Torres, for example, points out that the massive use of popular educators has prevented the bureaucratization of adult education efforts in Nicaragua; and that the most creative, committed, and nonauthoritarian teachers are found among these nonprofessionals.[18] She disdains the notion that the use of popular educators represents a valuable social experiment, a stopgap measure until adult educators are formally trained to meet professional certification standards.[19] Anecdotal material and observations from Torres' monograph, however, undercut her argument. A teacher-animator interviewed on the radio program *Puño en Alto* notes that "he would like to continue helping his CEP companions but he has exhausted the little capacity he has." As Torres notes, in effect, this literate *campesino*, by level three of EPB, had reached the limits not only of his pedagogical abilities but his information in the areas of natural sciences, history, geography, mathematics and grammar.[20]

The abilities of popular educators appear to be stretched beyond the breaking point. Approximately 50 percent of urban CEPs and 90 percent of rural CEPs involve heterogeneous grouping of students at different ability levels; and beginning in 1985, nine levels of education would be offered in CEPs with specialized subject matter from level five on.

In the face of these challenges, there have been extraordinary efforts by a substantial number of popular educators to upgrade their knowledge and improve their teaching skills. Even with constant upgrading, beginning with inservice training of popular educators between November 1982 and February 1983, it is unlikely that they will have adequate knowledge to teach beyond the introductory levels of EPB (one through four), which is where more than two-thirds of the students are found. Moreover, a pedagogy based on notions of dialogue and active inquiring learners requires unusually gifted teachers. Yet, according to the National Network in Solidarity with the Nicaraguan People, "Because many rural teachers are newly literate and there is an urgency to complete the exercise books and advance to higher levels of literacy, workshops for popular educators tend to focus more on the use of materials than on pedagogy and participation."[21]

Since 1983, there has been an emphasis on pedagogy as well. The ideal characteristics of EPB pedagogy articulated by former Vice-Minister of Adult Education Fransico Lacayo—that is, a scientific and efficacious teaching-learning methodology that at the same time is agile and flexible[22]—may be too much to ask of the average popular educator. Settling for a straightforward pedagogy that accomplishes the basic job of developing essential mathematical and language skills and providing a clear picture of national priorities may be a more reasonable expectation.

The best instruction I witnessed out of some 50 CEPs I had visited on different occasions over a three-year period took place in a sixth-level mathematics course, where the popular teacher was a university science student preparing to become a teacher. The instructor was systematic in his approach, clear in his explanations, and required each student to accurately perform a mathematical task—in this case, the law of equal proportions.

While teacher-centered pedagogy is something that I normally do not advocate, after comparing a number of CEPs with the Ministry of Education's more traditional accelerated primary education program (CEDA),[23] I came away with the impression that there is a lot to be said for systematic education that involves the transmission of large amounts of information in a didactic way. This type of instruction will not contribute to the goal of a more participatory culture, but it will contribute to another basic goal of popular education—to increase the level of knowledge and skills of people so as to further the material progress of the country.

Dropout and Burnout

In order to achieve this goal it will not only be necessary to recruit more knowledgeable and skilled teachers for the upper levels of EPB, but to retain and promote greater numbers of students in the system of adult education. According to Ministry of Planning data, of the 105,827 students in the first level of EPB in 1982, only 47 percent reached the third level by 1983; and between March and December 1983, approximately one-fourth of the students either dropped out of the program or failed to pass the examinations required to advance to the next level. In 1982–83, between 70 and 75 percent of all EPB students enrolled in the introductory course in basic literacy and the first two levels.

Besides the problems of substantial attrition and disruptions in regular attendance wrought by the defense and production mobilizations, EPB has begun to manifest the problems of more traditional adult education programs around the world. Whether or not the malaise may be attributed to institutionalization or creeping bureaucratization,[24] the fact is that sustaining the interests of learners five nights a week, week after week, over a number of years is extremely difficult. This is the case even in a revolutionary society and perhaps even more so due to the demands placed on ordinary citizens to participate in a variety of community and national tasks. Most of the participants, whether adolescents or adults, work during the day and often arrive at the CEPs exhausted.

Over time attendance begins to drop off. Inclement weather or any other inconvenience is sufficient excuse not to go to class. On the rainy night in June 1984 that I was scheduled to visit CEPs in working class neighborhoods of Managua, only one of four was functioning—and this center had been apprized that an outside guest and VIMEDA supervisors would be visiting.

Burnout and dropout is common among popular teachers as well. One-fourth of popular educators leave EPB on an annual basis.

The popular educators are largely volunteer labor. The 300 *cordobas* (28.5 *cordobas* to one US dollar at official rates in 1984) popular teachers receive, and the 500 cordobas supervisors receive, are used to cover transportation, food, and material costs of instruction. The popular educators, therefore, are primarily engaged in adult education efforts out of commitment and not for reasons of material gain. The same must be said of students who stay with their courses. As a *campesino* woman in Estelí observed, "Sometimes I just think, why should I be struggling with these books when I am so old? But now that I've started reading, even the newspaper, I feel like I've come to a new country and started all over again."[25]

The question raised by Fagen with regard to the transformation of political culture in Cuba is pertinent to Nicaragua: How does a political regime maintain high levels of sacrifice in a post-revolutionary period?[26] As in other countries following the path of revolution, the question of the proper mix of moral and material incentives arises.[27] In Nicaragua, a combination of incentives is being utilized to sustain a high level of effort in both the work force and in the social service sector. "Emulation," based on groups and individuals attempting to excel in some socially useful task, has been instituted in the education system as well. Various material prizes are awarded to CEPs at the district, regional, and national levels that have been exemplary in attendance, achievement, and promotion rates. Prizes for popular educators include books, clothing, food items that might be considered luxuries (e.g. canned tuna). And there is constant reinforcement of adult education efforts by the mass organizations. In factories where the Sandinista Workers' Central (CST) is strong, there is given time off from work and union encouragement to attend classes. The same is true of the 81 state agricultural enterprises, each of which has an adult education program. Similarly, the ATC and UNAG place great emphasis on encouraging the continuing education of their membership as vital to the activities of their organizations. And the 15,000 CDs each have a person responsible for educational affairs.

Articulation with Schooling and Workplace

A major concern of educational policymakers is what the graduates of the upper levels of EPB will be able to do with their education. As mentioned earlier, many of the younger students view EPB as a stepping stone to further formal education and certification, which will place a heavy load on the already over-taxed secondary education system. In 1984, the national inservice training system in *Sistema Nacional de Formación Profesional (SINAFORP)* also had limited capacity to absorb graduates of the fifth and sixth levels of EPB. In Managua, for example, SINAFORP training centers could accommodate only 400 of some 2,500 CEP graduates who were seeking technical training.[28]

The nature and future direction of adult education, therefore, has aroused serious concern among members of the Ministry of Education, the Ministry of Planning (which oversees educational policy in relation to economic and social plans of the nation), and the leadership of the FSLN.

It is probable that adult education at upper levels will be more related to vocational-skill training and take place in work sites for shorter periods. While the top political and educational leadership of the country is systematically grappling with these issues, another aspect of adult education is the object of intense debate among different political forces in the country.

Political Content of Popular Education

The most controversial issue surrounding education is the pro-FSLN content. It remains to be seen whether or not the content is modified to satisfy opposition groups that gained a measure of power in the November 1984 elections, winning 35 of the 96 seats in the National Assembly.[29]

As V.O. Key noted, "All national educational systems indoctrinate the oncoming generation with the basic outlooks and values of the political order. . . ."[30] Yet, Sandinista political goals transcend mere indoctrination. According to repeated pronouncements of the Sandinista leadership, popular education is designed "to create a nation of not only literate, but critical revolutionaries."[31] Passive acceptance and repetition of Sandinista slogans is not adequate. If a new culture and society are to be forged in the crucible of revolution, the prime movers of social change must be the very people who are the beneficiaries. The previous objects of history are to become its shakers and movers.

If these professed aims of the Sandinista revolution are taken at face value, then, there would appear to be a fundamental contradiction between pedagogical practice and the philosophy that is supposed to inspire educational effort. Despite the desired goal of a popular education system based on dialogue, analysis, and reflective social action, what frequently obtains, instead, is one-way, top-down transmission of political messages that are not questioned but are to be acted upon. This type of pedagogy conforms to what Freire has called the "banking" approach to education. It is a pedagogy that clearly does not facilitate the internalization of principles, nor the creative transformation of reality.

For the reasons discussed above, the efficacy of EPB as an agency of political socialization is problematic. Its greatest impact may reside, as with the CNA, in mobilizing previously disadvantaged groups (notably women, peasants, and youth) into important roles where they can contribute to the commonwealth. And not unlike the CNA, those who are likely to learn and change the most are the very teachers or "popular educators" themselves.

EPB is but one agency of nonformal education and political socialization.[32] Over 20 state agencies and mass organizations, as well as the mass media, are involved in popular education and the creation of a new political culture. These organizations are also the locus of some of the most important experiments taking place to give new direction to nonformal and adult education.

NEW TRENDS IN EPB

Some of the most promising innovations in adult education appear to reside in revamping the structure of EPB and relating it more directly to productive labor. The Ministry of Agricultural Development and Land Reform (MIDINRA) has taken the lead in designing innovative popular education programs. At the state-run Benjamín Zeledón Sugar Mill in Carazo, MIDINRA has established a course for "cultural advancement." The program enrolls individuals who have completed at least the first two levels of EPB and requires them to study full time for 45 days (with pay). In that time, participants complete the third through fifth levels of EPB. Another program being initiated at other centers of MIDINRA enrolls members of the state agricultural enterprises in training courses of short duration that take students with a basic education (approximately the fifth or sixth levels of EPB) and impart a specific technical skill that accords with national economic priorities.

Another innovation of EPB involves developing self-instructional materials or basic education texts such as *Caminemos* that contain answers to various questions and exercises. These materials are used in conjunction with defense and production mobilizations; and it is often the responsibility of the army and other state and mass organizations to assist with adult education activities that necessarily must occur outside the framework of the CEPs. It is to these other agencies and organizations that the analysis now turns.

STATE AGENCIES AND MASS ORGANIZATIONS IN POPULAR EDUCATION

In addition to actively supporting EPB, these state and mass organizations have instituted their own education divisions to upgrade the level of technical knowledge and organizational skills of their staffs and membership, and raise their political consciousness. Almost all are involved in training popular educators who serve as change agents (community and union organizers) involved in disseminating vital information on a mass basis in the areas of health and nutrition, women's and workers' rights, occupational safety, land reform and cooperatives, civil defense, and current events of national import. All, using the model of the CNA, employ some pyramidal form to train progressively larger numbers of people from the national level down to the municipal and community levels. For example, beginning with a group of approximately 15 high-level technical staff in Managua, UNAG eventually reaches and imparts knowledge about the philosophy and practice of cooperatives to representatives of some 1,000 cooperatives throughout the country. The Sandinista Army (EPS) uses a multiplier chain to ensure that there is one individual for every eight or ten soldiers at the brigade level who is responsible for political education. This education may focus on a contemporary issue—such as the pastoral letter in the spring of 1984 calling upon the Sandinista government to negotiate with the *contras*; or it may consist of sessions to help orient soldiers from the Pacific Coast to the culture of the Atlantic Coast.[33]

An excellent illustration of empowering people to provide a basic social service is the popular health program of the Ministry of Health (MINSA). The mass mobilizations to immunize people against malaria, polio, and other endemic diseases have involved more than 70,000 volunteers for short periods.[34] On a more permanent basis, MINSA has established a program of popular health education and services whereby every CDS is supposed to designate one person in a community to be responsible for the area of health; this person, in turn, is to be supported by a committee of CDS members. These community-level committees are concerned with identifying local health problems and launching educational and self-help efforts to improve living conditions.[35] District level offices of MINSA (backed by a national staff of 30) provide necessary training, information, and supplies when a national campaign is afoot. While the CDS serves as the axis for a number of mobilizations in health, other mass organizations play important supporting roles. AMNLAE, for example, has its own health teams that educate with regard to nutrition and health care; and it further contributed 5,000 members to work in the national immunization campaigns.

Furthermore, the mass organizations all have their own publications[36] that stress not only themes specific to their constituencies but the national themes of economic growth, anti-imperialism, national defense, and popular participation. In all these publications, the figure of Sandino looms large. This was particularly true in 1984, the 50th anniversary of his assassination.

As in EPB materials, the publications generally are easily readable and designed to appeal to the interests of a mass audience. They commonly use puzzles and anagrams, a variety of games using language skills; and they also employ elements of popular culture from different regions of the country, including folk tales and children's stories. Although reading materials are printed on inexpensive paper (frequently at newspaper presses), they are attractively illustrated with cartoon figures and photographs. The materials also receive high marks on use of everyday language to examine in straightforward terms complex social issues—such as food shortages and commodity speculation—and to deal with frequently circulating rumors about the causes of common problems. Although the perspective presented is that of the Sandinistas, issues are not skirted and mistakes committed by the government and mass organizations are admitted.

The creative use of the mass media and, above all, the visual arts (in billboards and murals) and the performing arts (theater, dance, musical ensembles) to disseminate political messages and raise consciousness is characteristic of the FSLN.[37] During the insurrection against Somoza, the music and song of Carlos and Luis Enrique Mejía Godoy instructed militants in the arts of warfare—how to assemble an M–1 carbine or how to manufacture a twine (*mecate*) bomb. Besides the outpouring of poetry, there has been a proliferation of theater groups that serve didactic purposes and provide entertainment for isolated communities as well as army units in battle zones. MECATE (*Movimiento de Expresión Campesina Artística Estatal*) involves 27 musical and nine theater groups of rural populations affiliated with the ATC and UNAG. Four hundred fifty teachers belonging to ANDEN have formed 35 groups of amateur artists. The Ministry of Culture and its program of Popular Cultural Centers (*Centros de Cultura Popular*—CPC) has provided instruction, guidance, and encouragement to between 18,000 and 20,000 amateur artists in the country in the areas of music, dance, plastic arts, theater, and poetry.[38] Almost invariably the goal is the revival of popular forms of artistic expression, the development of national culture, and the linkage of that culture to a new political and social order.[39]

Notable among the efforts to develop national art forms that entertain as well as instruct politically are those of the Nicaraguan Film Institute (INCINE). By 1984, INCINE had produced 46 short subject (15–20 minutes), 14 half-hour, and two feature-length films. Sixteen of the films had won international awards. All the films have aesthetic as well as political purposes. Besides documenting the various challenges to and achievements of the present political regime, they are designed to raise levels of political awareness and participation.

INCINE has 35 mobile units which travel to the most remote areas of the country,[40] including the war zones, to show not only their own productions but a variety of film classics from other countries. Humor is combined with political commentary. Comedies of Charlie Chaplin and Harold Lloyd are shown along with films of Buñuel, Eisenstein, and Gutiérrez Alea. After each film showing, audience members are encouraged to discuss their reactions to what they viewed. It is not uncommon for 25 people (including children) out of an audience of 200 to express their opinions on what they liked and did not like and why. INCINE estimates that as of 1984, approximately 1.5 (or one half the country's population) million spectators viewed their films. As is the case with other forms of popular education, the projectionist-discussion leaders are usually from working-class and peasant backgrounds and have been trained on the job.

Various mass organizations also have their own weekly radio programs. These include AMNLAE's *Somos* (We Are), ATC's *Surco* (Furrow), and the Ministry of Culture's *CPC Aquí Presente* (CPCs Present). Moreover, there is a weekly radio program devoted to the music and popular culture of the Atlantic Coast. The twice daily broadcast of EPB, *Puño en Alto,* and the weekly popular education page and topical education campaigns of the Sandinista newspaper *Barricada,* as well as the two Sandinista controlled television channels, all provide systematic and repetitive reinforcement of the same national messages.

At the neighborhood level, the block Sandinista Defense Committees further reinforce the messages of the FSLN vanguard. In workplaces, unions and employee associations are constantly calling meetings to exhort workers to higher levels of production, to alert them to U.S. aggression, or explain why there are shortages of consumer items and how they will be distributed. In 1984, the image of Sandino was omnipresent—his silhouette painted on walls, sidewalks, buildings—and different work sites had competitions concerning "who knew more about Sandino." In accordance with notions of socialist emulation, different work-unit teams vied with each other to answer questions such as these: "What were the historical circumstances that motivated the resistance of Sandino?" "Compare the conduct of oligarchic dominant groups during the epoch of Sandino (1927–33) with what they are presently doing in the context of the counterrevolution." "What is the project that the CIA directs and finances by means of the counterrevolution?"[41]

While it would seem that the activities of the FSLN, various state entities, and mass organizations in the areas of popular education and political socialization are well coordinated, consistent, and comprehensive, this is far from being an accurate picture. The following sections describe some of the problems confronting nonformal education programs at the level of state agencies, mass organizations, and the mass media.

PROBLEMS AND CONTRADICTIONS OF NONFORMAL EDUCATION

The principal inconsistencies and contradictions of nonformal education derive from the following factors. There is a lack of coordination, if not rivalry, among the various organizations involved in popular education. The allocation of human resources depends on market mechanisms, which may not accord with state priorities. Political and cultural pluralism exists alongside efforts to create a political culture according to certain predefined notions. Traditional cultural patterns co-exist with a revolutionary situation that places new demands on people and expects them to act in new ways. Finally, there is an emphasis by the Sandinista leadership on a participatory political culture with critical, inquiring citizens while a vanguard, the FSLN, frequently dictates action to nonquestioning mass organizations and individuals.

One of the clearest examples of lack of interorganizational cooperation involves the two workshops organized by MIDINRA and the Agrarian Education and Promotion Center (CEPA)[42] for 19 different ministries, religious groups, and mass organizations in June 1983 and 1984 to discuss techniques used by the different agencies for training popular educators and making their work more effective. Noticeably absent were representatives of the Ministry of Education and particularly the Vice-Ministry of Adult Education. MIDINRA, which has pioneered innovative programs in adult education and labor-force training, was only beginning to sit down with MED and VIMEDA officials in June 1984 to discuss extension of these programs. MIDINRA and UNAG on certain occasions had suggested to personnel of the Ministry of Education changes in the vocabulary of EPB materials that were more appropriate for rural populations—for example, terms referring to units of measurement—but as of mid-1984, they still had not worked out arrangements for the possibility of publishing materials at the more advanced levels of EPB that were specifically geared to the interests of their members in improving agricultural and industrial production and learning needed technical and organizational skills.

SINAFORP, the national inservice training organization of the Ministry of Labor, is a patent example of centralized efforts giving way to decentralized education programs. SINAFORP, having lost a power struggle, was to be effectively phased out of training activities by the end of 1984. In place of SINAFORP, each ministry (for example, Construction, Telecommunications, Energy) was to employ its own training staff and conduct its own inservice upgrading activities. It remains to be seen whether or not SINAFORP and the Ministry of Education will play active roles in establishing guidelines and supervising the more decentralized system.

The case of SINAFORP suggests that rivalries do occur. Within the FSLN and across different state and mass organizations, there is considerable discussion and disagreement as to exactly what new form EPB should take, as well as how best to prepare an adequately skilled and politically consciouess work force.

While there is a National Ministry of Planning (MIPLAN), and the state has nationalized banking, mining, and international commerce,

Nicaragua has a mixed economy with a large private sector. In 1984, 60 percent of the economy was in private hands, and the private sector accounted for 75 percent of all commercial and agricultural production; it also received 70 percent of all public investment funds. As Conroy notes, "Market pricing and allocation determine the vast majority of all economic decisions within the country. Although minimum wages have been established for all areas and all types of work, there has been no attempt to plan, allocate, or otherwise organize labour markets in the form that characterizes the actually existing socialist countries. . . ."[43]

The implications for education, both formal and nonformal, are that it has been difficult for the Ministry of Education as well as other public agencies to retain teachers, who may be offered higher-paying jobs in the private sector. Markets in labor also suggest that there may not be strong linkage between government economic plans and training programs and actual utilization of skills.

Notions of professionalism also are difficult to change. The health sector is typical of the difficulties involved in changing old attitudes concerning who has the right to exercise what activities vital to an individual's well being. Traditional notions are particularly well engrained among older physicians. Advocates of empowering people with skills and knowledge, normally monopolized by health professionals, remain critical of the current situation in Nicaragua. They laud the Sandinista government for its popular health programs that are built on broad-scale participation and the idea that health is the responsibility of all; and they compare the current situation of health care in Nicaragua favorably with other Central American countries. But they also believe that there is still too much emphasis on a clinical, curative, and professionally-dominated approach rather than on a preventative, more holistic approach to health.[44]

Post-1979 Nicaragua is characterized not only by a mixed economy but by cultural pluralism. Although the government controls the two extant television channels, a majority of the country's radio stations in 1984 (23 of 39) were privately owned. Despite the efforts of the government and the mass organizations to promote indigenous culture, a survey of radio program content conducted by the Ministry of Culture found that less than 10 percent of music broadcasting consisted of traditional folk music or educational programming and over 70 percent consisted of popular rock and roll or disco music from abroad. Moreover, television programming is saturated with soap operas from other Latin American countries that have prime-time billing and attract large audiences. These soap operas, such as the Venezuelan series based on the life of the dictator Juan Vicente Gómez, may examine the dynamics of a repressive political order but they also concentrate inordinately on the life style of the upper class and bourgoisie, romanticizing their existence in contradistinction to the emphases of the Sandinista leadership on highlighting the virtues of the working class and peasantry. Although advertising that is exploitative or denigrating to women has been prohibited by law, many of the television sociodramas portray women in traditional, subordinate roles or as mere objects of beauty. AMNLAE has protested such series as the Brazilian drama, *Isaura the Slave,* and may take a stronger stand in the future on the values portrayed by the soap operas.

To queries concerning inconsistencies found in television programming, the Vice-Minister of Culture, Francisco Lacayo, forcefully states that the government has no intention of imposing a "stupid cultural dictatorship."[45] Furthermore, as he points out, Nicaragua is open to all currents of international culture to an unprecedented extent. This international thrust of cultural policy complements current emphases on the conservation and dissemination of national culture.

People seek entertainment and perhaps escape from the turmoil of everyday existence. Instead, they are constantly bombarded by exhortation in the mass media, workplace, and community to contribute their spare time to defense activities, increased production, and neighborhood improvement. There may be a boomerang effect from the Sandinistas' use of the political "harangue" and what they call *dosificación* to raise political consciousness, to remind people of the internal and external threats they face, especially directed at urban populations about sacrifices being made by those in the war zones and those involved in military duty. There is the distinct probability of overkill, of people "turning-off." Even well motivated individuals may not want to sit through another meeting or listen to another speech after a long day of work. The Sandinista Youth Association, as a case in point, published a bulletin discussing the concerns of youths regarding the JS–19 J, one of the principal concerns was the inordinate number of hours spent in meetings. The bulletin reassures readers that instead of endless meetings, there is but one per month.[46]

The mass organizations, which are the mechanisms for mobilizing the population around the tasks of the revolution, are in many instances little more than forums for transmitting the political line being propounded by the FSLN at any given moment. However, this is not always the case. The ATC, for example, has organized sit-ins at government offices of state-run enterprises, when it felt that workers' rights were not being honored or promises being fulfilled. Similarly, unions have aired their dissatisfaction with certain state economic policies through various job actions. Moreover, the mass organizations are not beholden to the government for their financial support, which comes from membership dues and contributions. Nonetheless, all the mass organizations with semi-official status, in terms of representation on state legislative or policy councils, recognize the FSLN as a "vanguard" organization and are obligated in their constitutions to follow its lead.

The top-down transmission of policy and political messages (propaganda) finds its counterpart in the workplace and block CDS meetings that are a part of everyday existence. It is not uncommon for those attending meetings to be lectured to for an hour or more by different FSLN representatives. After sitting through such a CDS meeting in a working-class neighborhood of Managua, a staff member of the national office of the CDS observed enthusiastically, "You can see there is a lot of participation." What I had observed was some 30 people sitting for about 45 minutes in fold-up chairs in the early evening dusk while three different FSLN spokesmen read to them nationally-prepared statements on the causes of the economic problems in the country; there had not been a single question or comment from the group assembled in the street.

The goal of achieving critical consciousness is tempered by the desire of a vanguard to present what it sees as the current interpretation of a particular historical situation or moment—*coyuntura*. As in China, with the mass line propounded by the Chinese Communist Party, it is possible to argue that a vanguard learns from the people; analyzes existing situations from the vantage point of scientific principles and a long-term historical perspective; articulates what needs to be done to overcome current impasses, problems, and contradictions; and then returns to the mass base to test the validity of its prescriptions. The experience from China, as well as from the Soviet Union and Eastern Europe, is that this process frequently degenerates into party functionaries or bureaucrats dictating in an authoritarian fashion to the population at large.

Still, there is a vibrancy and openness to much of the political discussion and policy formulation in Nicaragua. The openness can be seen in government leaders on a periodic basis (usually weekly) going to different communities in the country and in a public forum, *Cara al Pueblo* ("Face to Face with the People"), which is televised for national broadcast, entertaining any and all comments and criticisms. These forums have been characterized by surprising candor on the part of both public and government officials.

In the formulation and interpretation of public policy in education, as in other areas, divergent points of view vie with one another. There is no rigid orthodoxy. The FSLN itself has undergone shifts in ideological focus and emphasis, with different factions ascendant at different points in its evolution.[47]

The tumultuous changes the country has been undergoing, plus the foreign aggression against it, has at times led to both rapid shifts in policy and inconsistencies in policy implementation. During the national election year of 1984, for example, a FSLN commitment to freedom of expression by all contending political parties in the country clashed with deep-seated contempt for the historical role that the traditional parties had played in maintaining the country in a dependent status *vis-à-vis* the United States and in perpetuating an unjust status quo. Suspicion on the part of the Sandinistas of the patriotism of these parties was reinforced by the continuing support certain factions of the Conservative and Liberal Parties were giving to the counterrevolutionaries and to U.S. intervention in the affairs of the country.

Even the ubiquitous emphasis on Sandino as a nationalist, populist hero who fought against foreign intervention and championed Latin American unity in the face of the Colossus of the North may have contradictory consequences. While it is the intention of certain FSLN ideologues that the figure of Sandino serve as a point of identification with the FSLN and ultimately with socialism, the historical Sandino does not exactly fit the mold of Marxism-Leninism. An identification with Sandino and Sandinismo may simply reinforce patriotic sentiments in Nicaraguans. Moreover, there is much in the writings and philosophy of Sandino that would also reinforce mysticism and romantic indigenism—tendencies not in accordance with the Sandinistas political ideology.

The very notion of political consciousness is subject to different interpretation by various mass organizations involved in education and social action—a reflection of the considerable political and cultural pluralism that exists in the society. Many of the religious groups involved in popular education creatively combine interpretation of Christianity with elements of class analysis and anti-imperialism derived from Marxism and Leninism. Organizations such as CEPAD (the Evangelical Committee to Promote Development) and the CEPA (the Agrarian Education and Promotion Center) are driven by a vision of a more just society while leaving the definition of the exact nature of that society open-ended. Generally, much of the leadership of the FSLN is also characterized by both flexibility and pragmatism concerning the nature of the road to development and a realization that politics is the art of the possible.

SUMMARY

Questions raised at the end of the 1980 national literacy crusade also pertain to the follow-up programs of EPB and the ongoing nonformal education activities of state agencies, mass organizations, and the mass media. It remains to be seen whether or not the newly acquired skills of literacy and the basic education imparted in a variety of programs will be successfully applied to increasing economic productivity, better health, more adequate housing, and effective communal action. With fewer than half the students who participated in the CNA entering and completing even the first two levels of EPB, and with constant disruptions in education programs (largely due to the aggression against the country), as well as the high dropout rate, a substantial number of adults may lapse into illiteracy or simply retain a minimal level of literacy[48] that is not adequate to the increasing demands placed upon the Nicaraguan citizenry. But because of these demands for more skilled, informed, and participatory citizens—and because of the opportunities opened by the revolution—it is very much the case that tens of thousands of previously illiterate and poorly skilled individuals are now playing important roles at all levels of the society, from co-op to national legislative bodies.

A related question pertains to the balance between the twin goals of skill training and consciousness raising. At times, emphasis has been placed on political education to the detriment of imparting basic language and computational skills and necessary technical knowledge. Moreover, pedagogical practice frequently has taken the form of crude indoctrination which does not raise the kind of critical awareness according to which individuals willingly choose courses of action. If the faith must be practiced, it must also, according to the tenets of Sandinismo, be internalized, understood, and consciously put into practice by its adherents.

Yet, to concentrate on the limitations and weaknesses of popular education in Nicaragua is to do injustice to what in so many respects is a truly innovative and exciting set of programs and activities. The sight of formerly illiterate peasants teaching their own family and neighbors, of 13-year-old youths teaching even younger peers, of grandparent and grandchild studying together at night, of people who reverently carry with them to class the collected poems of Rubén Darío because they know that some day they will be able to read them, the confidence and self-assertion of formerly mute peasants and workers, the new roles they play in areas vital to their lives, the artistic outpouring that issues forth from the host of adult education programs—all this is inspirational! Whatever the shortcomings of EPB, the achievements are also remarkable.

The future direction and nature of popular education remains unclear. In many respects, EPB, like the national literacy crusade, was conceived primarily as a "political project with pedagogical implications,"[49] rather than as an education project with political consequences. There is the problem of conceptualizing the nature of a system of post-literacy education, when "literacy itself was not in principle conceived of as adult education."[50]

Whether or not EPB will succumb to the bureaucratization that has overcome other adult education efforts around the world, and whether or not it will eventually be subordinated to an increasing demand for formal schooling remain open questions. A final set of questions relates to the impact of popular education on the formal education system: to what extent have the innovative practices of the literacy campaign and EPB influenced the new school system that emerged in the fall of 1980? And to what extent has schooling changed in Sandinista Nicaragua? We turn to these questions in the next chapter.

NOTES

1. MED, *Política y Lineamientos del Desarrollo Educativo dentro del Plan Nacional de Desarrollo de la Educación No Superior de Nicaragua a Mediano Plazo, (1984–1990)* (Managua: Ministry of Education/General Division of Planning, 1983), p. 20.

2. For further discussion of land reform policies of the FSLN, see Joseph R. Thome and David Kaimowitz, "Agrarian Reform," in *Nicaragua: The First Five Years,* ed. Thomas W. Walker (New York: Praeger, 1985), pp. 299–315.

3. When UNAG was formed in April 1981 thousands of members of ATC, who had become property owners because of land reform, joined the new mass organization. Thus, the membership of ATC dropped considerably.

4. "Report of the Latin American Studies Association Delegation to Observe the Nicaraguan General Election of November 4, 1985," *LASA Forum* 15 (Winter 1985): 15.

5. According to Joseph Collins with Francis Moore Lappé, Nick Allen and Paul Rice, *What Difference Could a Revolution Make? Food and Farming in the New Nicaragua* (San Francisco: Institute for Food and Development Policy, 1985 edition), p. 50, the ATC by May 1982 had organized 25 workshops to help farm workers detect and deal with decapitalization. They note that the Sandinista newspaper *Barricada* commented, "In the private sector workers are pressuring more and more to penetrate the 'secrets' of production."

6. Interview with Magda Enríquez, then head of education and propaganda of AMNLAE, in Managua, May 25, 1984.

7. Edgar Macías Gómez, "Análisis de la Estructura y Funcionamiento del Sistema Nacional de Eduación de Adultos," in *Educación y Dependencia,* ed. by INPRHU (Managua: Instituto de Promoción Humana, 1976), p. 135.

8. Ibid., p. 184.

9. Ibid., p. 168.

10. See, for example, MED, *Proposiciones para Establecer la Filosofía, los Objectivos, las Lineas de Acción y la Estructura de la "EDA" en Nicaragua para Contribuir al Proceso de la Reconstrucción Nacional* (Managua: Ministry of Education, Department of Primary Education, July 1979), pp. 2, 9.

11. Deborah Barndt, "Popular Education," in *Nicaragua,* Walker (ed.), p. 320.

12. For discussion of these concepts and different paradigms for viewing education and development, see Rolland Paulston, "Social and Educational Change: Conceptual Frameworks," *Comparative Education Review* 21 (June/October 1977): 370–94; Jerome Karabel and A.H. Halsey, "Educational Research: A Review and an Interpretation," in their edited collection, *Power and Ideology in Education* (New York: Oxford University Press, 1977), pp. 1–86; Gail P. Kelly, Philip G. Altbach, and Robert F. Arnove, "Trends in Comparative Education: A Critical Analysis," in *Comparative Education,* eds. Altbach, Arnove, and Kelly (New York: Macmillan, 1982), pp. 509–19; and in the same edited collection, John C. Bock, "Education and Development: A Conflict of Meanings," pp. 78–101.

13. Torres, *Post-Alfabetización,* p. 23.

14. Francisco Lacayo, in *Primer Congreso Nacional de Educación Popular de Adultos* (Managua: Ministry of Education, June 1981), p. 36.

15. *Puño en Alto* ("Fist Raised High"—the Sandinista salute) was first broadcast during the CNA to upgrade the teaching skills of the *brigadistas* and provide useful advice on problems the literacy teachers were confronting.

16. National Network in Solidarity with the Nicaraguan People, "*Pueblo en Marcha*: Adult Education in Nicaragua," *Nicaragua,* October/November 1982 reprinted in *The Nicaragua Reader,* ed. Peter Rosset and John Vandermeer (New York: Grove Press, 1983), p. 338.

17. Ibid.

18. Torres, *Post-Alfabetización,* pp. 26–8.

19. Ibid., p. 28.

20. Ibid., p. 24.

21. National Network in Solidarity with the Nicaraguan People, "Adult Education," p. 338.

22. Lacayo, Speech in *Educación Popular de Adultos,* p. 34.

23. CEDA enables urban populations over the age of 16 to earn a primary school diploma in three years instead of the normal period of 6 years. Teachers in the program are usually Ministry of Education employees who teach during the day in the formal school system and who work at night in CEDA for supplementary pay.

24. The problem of bureaucratization is discussed extensively in Torres, *Post-Alfabetización* and in the speech by Francisco Lacayo at the Primer Congreso Nacional de Educación Popular de Adultos, pp. 33–38.

25. National Network in Solidarity with the Nicaraguan People, "Adult Education," p. 340.

26. Fagen, *Transformation of Political Culture,* p. 164.

27. For further discussion of moral and material incentives, see, for example, Robert M. Bernardo, "Moral Stimulation as a Non-Market Mode of Labor Allocation in Cuba," *Studies in Comparative International Development,* Vol. 6, no. 6 (New Brunswick, N.J.: Rutgers University, 1970–71): 119–38.

28. Interview with William Villagre, General Director of SINAFORP, Managua, May 30, 1984.

29. For further discussion, see LASA, "Report of Delegation."

30. V.O. Key, Jr., *Public Opinion and American Democracy* (New York: Knopf, 1961), p. 316.

31. National Network in Solidarity with the Nicaraguan People, "Adult Education," p. 338.

32. Interview with Ernesto Vallecillo, Vice-Minister of Adult Education, VIMEDA, Managua, June 11, 1984.

33. The Nicaraguan Permanent Commission on Human Rights also regularly visits on weekends different army bases to educate soldiers as to the human and legal rights of prisoners, and how Sandinista policy toward the rights of prisoners differ from that of the Somoza regime. Interview with Miguel Angel Aviles, director of the Permanent Commission on Human Rights, at CNES (National Higher Education Council), June 13, 1984.

34. For further discussion on the subject, see David C. Halpern and Richard Garfield, "Developments in Health Care in Nicaragua," *New England Journal of Medicine* 307 (1982): 33–92. However, it should be noted that because of the internal and external aggression against Nicaragua and the shortage of funds for so-

cial service programs, national investments in mass-scale inoculations against polio and other diseases has had to be cut back.

35. MINSA, "Jornadas Popular de Salud" (Managua: Ministry of Health, 1981).

36. The magazines include *Somos* of AMNLAE, which grew from an 8-page publication with a circulation of 2,000 to 24 pages and a circulation of 25,000 by 1984; *El Machete* of ATC; and *Chahalaga* and the bulletin "La Pluma" of the Centers of Popular Culture.

37. The sophisticated use of art work, advertising techniques, and the mass media by the FSLN was evident during the 1984 national election campaign. The FSLN's publicity was much more appealing and "with it"—even when they used only a swatch of red and black paint on walls—to advertise their party.

38. Interview with Julio Sandaño, national headquarters of CPC, Managua, June 6, 1984.

39. Interview with Francisco Lacayo, Vice-Minister of Culture, Managua, May 23, 1984.

40. According to Rodolfo Alegría, head of international relations of IN-CINE, the institute's mobile unit program is aimed at reaching the most isolated areas of the country and therefore does not show films in Managua and its environs. Interview at INCINE, Managua, June 14, 1984.

41. UNE (National Union of Employees)/CNES (National Higher Education Council) Segundo Concurso, Quién Sabe Mas Sobre Sandino? May 1984.

42. CEPA (Centro de Educación y Promoción Agraria) was organized by Jesuits in the mid-1970s and is one of five such organizations in Central America that work in skill training and consciousness raising among disadvantaged sectors of society. For further discussion, see Barndt, "Popular Education," p. 322.

43. Michael E. Conroy, "False Polarisation? Different Perspectives on the Economic Strategies of Post-Revolutionary Nicaragua, *Third World Quarterly* 6 (October 1984): 1018.

44. This perspective characterizes the work of the Centro de Información y Servicios de Asesoría en Salud, (CISAS), located in Managua.

45. Lacayo interview, see n. 39.

46. Juventud Sandinista 19 de Julio, "Sabes lo que Pasa en la JS-19 de Julio" (Managua: same, 1981).

47. For further discussion, see David Nolan, *FSLN* (Coral Gables: Institute of Interamerican Studies, University of Miami, 1984). For a different perspective, see Deirdre English, "We Are Sandinistas: Conversations with Nicaragua's Embattled Leaders," *Mother Jones,* (August/September 1985): 22–28, 51.

48. According to MIPLAN/Department of Social Planning information, in 1984, there were approximately 250,000 "residual" illiterates in the country not reached by the program of permanent literacy.

49. Roberto Saenz, Program Director of VIMEDA, cited in Hirshon, *And Teach Them to Read,* p. 7; similar statement made by the first Minister of Education, Carlos Tünnermann Bernheim, in Philip Zwerling and Connie Martin, *Nicaragua—A New Kind of Revolution* (Westport, Conn.: Lawrence Hill, 1985), p. 67.

50. Quotation cited in Torres, *Post-Alfabetización,* p. 26.

4
Primary and Secondary Schooling: Achievements, Limitations, and Contradictions

Based on new notions of the relation between education and national development, since 1979 preuniversity education has been expanded, improved in many respects, and generally reordered. Changes reflect the socioeconomic goals of satisfying basic necessities and raising the standard of living, overcoming Nicaragua's dependent position in the world economic system, and establishing a new model of economic accumulation.[1] Schooling and nonformal education programs are called upon to prepare people with the knowledge, skills, values, and predispositions to play more active roles in an economy governed by the "logic of the majority,"[2] and in a political system in which democracy is defined in terms of popular participation in national reconstruction.[3]

This chapter summarizes the preuniversity achievements of the Nicaraguan revolution during 1979–84. It also points out areas in which reforms have fallen short of expectations or are yet to be realized. Examples will be given of the problems which have emerged, the ways in which they have been addressed, and the consequences of decisions that, in turn, pose further challenges to the education establishment.

As is so frequently the case in societies undergoing radical change, the solution of one set of problems leads to the emergence of another set. Revolutionary situations where sweeping changes are made in telescoped periods are often characterized by contradictions. If dialectical materialism involves the search for unity in contradictions, then the revolutionary situation in Nicaragua has provided abundant opportunities for decision makers to engage in dialectical analysis.

73

EXPANSION

Nicaragua's primary and secondary education system has undergone a remarkable expansion. Overall, preuniversity educational enrollments nearly doubled between 1979 and 1984, from 477,869 to 891,391.

Enrollment expansion has been matched by the employment of a large number of teachers, many of whom were unable to find work during the Somoza period due to lack of opportunities and to discrimination against political opponents.

Table 4.1: Number of Students

	Preprimary	Primary	Secondary	Special Education
1978	9,000	369,640	98,874	355
1984	66,850	635,637	186,104	2,800

Table 4.2: Number of Teachers

	Preprimary	Primary	Secondary	Special Education
1978	——	9,986	2,720	——
1984	1,701	17,969	6,014	204

At the primary level, 5,920 new teacher places have been created. The number of normal schools in the country expanded from 5 to 14, with a total 1984 enrollment of 11,000. New careers were opened in preschool and special education, and a specialization in basic education (grades 1–4) was created.

During the first five years of the Sandinista government, 1,404 primary schools with 3,334 classrooms were built. The corresponding figures for secondary education are 48 secondary education centers and 692 classrooms. In the school construction program, the priority was extending primary education to the rural areas. At the secondary education level, emphasis was placed on building high schools in small cities and towns.

New technical and agricultural centers have been placed in what were the most neglected areas of the country. These centers include a fishing and navigation institute in Bluefields, a Mining Institute in Bonanza, a technical institute in Puerto Cabezas, and a forestry institute in San Ramón. The institutes have been built with credit lines provided by the USSR, the Federal and Democratic Republics of Germany, Sweden, and Spain.[4] Technical and agricultural education, which represented less than 0.1 percent of all secondary students prior to 1979, grew to over 8,000 students (approximately 5 percent of enrollments).

Financially, national allocations to the Ministry of Education have increased more than fourfold—from 346 million cordobas in 1979 to 1,403,894 in 1984. (The 1984 figure includes 168 million cordobas allocated to adult education.) Preuniversity education in 1984 represented approximately 4 percent of gross domestic product, as compared with 1.9 percent of GDP in 1979.

While the expansion of enrollments, teachers, and school facilities has been dramatic, there are serious constraints on the ability of the government to continue contributing as much to education as it did during the first five years of the revolution. Because defense expenditures consume at least 40 percent of the budget, allocations to the education and health sectors—and to all social services—as of 1985, were frozen at 1984 levels. Construction on 27 schools had to be stopped. Moreover, counterrevolutionary forces have wreaked considerable physical damage. In June 1984, the Ministry of Education (MED) estimated that 15 schools had been destroyed and another 138 had to be abandoned for security reasons.

Beyond the financial and material restraints, the expansion itself has generated problems. As in many countries, the opening of schools to previously excluded populations means a large influx of older students. In first grade classrooms, youths may range in age from 6 to 16. In Nicaragua, there were approximately 100,000 students in grades one through four at least three years older than what is considered the normal age. Solutions include encouraging students to enroll in various accelerated primary programs. However, the accelerated primary—which involves offering the standard curriculum in three years instead of six—may be too intense for a number of students and drive them out of the system.

One of the factors contributing to the large number of overage students was the low promotion rate of students in the first two years of primary. In 1982, for example, one-fourth of the entering students repeated first grade—one consequence being that 72 percent of first grade students were at least one year over age, and 51 percent were two or more years over age.

In order to improve this situation, the Ministry of Education, in 1983, instituted automatic promotion between grades one and two. Over the next three years, automatic promotion was to be progressively extended through grade four. It remains to be seen whether or not automatic promotion will lead to large numbers being passed on to higher grades without the requisite skills or necessitate large-scale remediation at the beginning of each school year and some form of ability grouping within classrooms, but the potential for these problems to occur is strong.

One major difference between the pre- and post-1979 school systems is that the majority of rural school children now attend school, while during the Somoza period three-fourths did not. However, despite the dramatic expansion of enrollments, the school completion rate remains low and not noticeably different from that of the Somoza epoch. The Ministry of Education's 1983 middle-range plan notes that only about 37 percent of urban children complete four years of schooling and in rural areas barely 7 percent.[5] In 1978, the last school year of the Somoza regime, only 6 percent of rural students completed sixth grade.

Prior to 1979, 65 percent of the relevant age group attended primary school (the vast majority of these students residing in urban areas); by 1984, that rate was approximately 80 percent with a goal of 85 percent for 1985. Still, in 1984, there were approximately 125,000 school-age youth not reached by formal education programs.

The ministry's goal that all Nicaraguan youth complete four years of primary schooling by 1990 may appear to be a modest one. But a number of people think that even this goal may not be realistic, given the material constraints on education. Other middle-range goals for the period 1985–90 include achieving a promotion rate of 77 percent and reducing repetition and dropout rates to 10–12 percent by 1990.[6]

Quantitative gains in and of themselves may be symbolically significant of government commitment to extend basic social services to the vast majority of the Nicaraguan population. However, without qualitative improvements in the content and methods of education, the desired economic and social outcomes of expanded schooling are unlikely to be realized.

IMPROVEMENTS

Among the principal improvements in education are the reorganization and decentralization of Ministry of Education activities; the elaboration and production of Nicaraguan educational materials; the development of a national educational publishing capacity; upgrading of school libraries, science laboratories, and craft workshops; the introduction of a new system of language instruction; the implementation of bilingual education for the Miskito-speaking populations of the Atlantic Coast; and the institution of programs and methods for the constant upgrading of the teaching force.

These reforms, in most cases, are in their incipient stages. As such, they all pose a number of problems and challenges. As indications of government intent to link innovations in schooling to changes in society, they also provide valuable insights into the promise and limitations of schooling.

Centralization and Decentralization

Since 1979, the state has played a major role in the planning and regulation of all levels and programmatic areas of education. What were largely privately-run and even proprietary interests—for example, preschool education, teacher training, technical and commercial education— are now primarily public functions and social utilities under the control of the Ministry of Education. What was a set of disaggregated educational activities, divorced from national economic development plans and popular welfare, is now viewed by MED officials as a more coherent and efficiently managed enterprise.

Private education still has an important role to play in Nicaraguan education. Church-related schools enroll a substantial number of students, particularly at the secondary level; and the best endowed schools at this level are found in the private sector. At the end of 1983, there were over 150,000 students in private education. In that year, 25 to 30 percent of all Nicaraguan students attended church schools[7] which were partially funded by the government. The Ministry of Education, in 1983, subsidized 114 private education centers for the sum of 61.1 million córdobas; this sum does not include further ministry assistance in the form of salaries or hourly wages paid to teachers working in them.[8]

Speaking of public aid to church-affiliated schools, Minister of Education Carlos Tünnermann Bernheim noted the following:

> When we have congregations that offer private schooling to the children, including children of the poor, then our ministry offers aid to pay the teachers and buy the books, even though the private administration hires the teachers and chooses the books. If the school teaches the approved curriculum, they are then free to teach whatever religious subjects they choose, and the state will pay for everything. So, in reality, the parents are free to choose the education they want for their children.[9]

Despite this framework for state-private sector cooperation in education, a substantial number of Nicaraguans are hostile to the efforts of the Sandinista government to develop and teach a common curriculum. Those opposed to the government view the new curriculum as an imposition of alien and antithetical principles and values. For its part, the government views education as an ideological apparatus of the state,[10] and, given the desired changes in Nicaraguan society, the vehicle for the dissemination of a new set of values and perceptions as to the nature of society and how change best occurs. Thus, the curriculum, as in almost all societies, is an arena of intense debate and conflict. The resolution of this debate pertains to the political domain and is part of the ongoing dialogue between the FSLN and major opposition groups in the country that is now taking place within the newly formed national assembly.

The centralizing tendencies in MED—most evident in the areas of planning, curriculum development, textbook production, and teacher training—are countered by significant decentralization in other areas. Beginning in May 1981, MED developed a proposal for the regionalization of education. This project was revised to accord with the July 1982 Decree of National Regionalization that organized the country into six political-administration regions and three special zones for the areas of Northern, Central, and Southern Zelaya (the Atlantic Coast). This regionalization, according to Barndt, "allowed for more direct participation in economic planning based on the productive capacity of a region. . . . This structure assured a more integral relationship between educational and economic projects. It also encouraged better coordination between educational programs and the work of mass organizations."[11]

NER: The combination of centralizing and decentralizing tendencies in education is reflected in the creation of administrative-educational networks, NER (rural education *núcleos*) that facilitate concentration of educational resources in base schools serving sub-base and satellite schools. Outlying satellite schools, consisting of one or two teachers and the first three or four years of instruction, are supposed to feed students into the sub-base schools for the upper primary grades. The base schools offer the full complement of primary and first cycle secondary education, with workshops, better endowed libraries and laboratories, and specialized personnel to meet the needs of a large geographical area. The networks are supposed to be designed so no satellite is more than six to seven kilometers from a sub-base, and sub-base schools no more than 15 kilometers from the base school.[12] In 1984, there were 24 NER with a total of 257 schools, 956 teachers, and 32,232 students. As will be discussed in a subsequent section on transformations in education, the NER are an agency for bringing state, mass organizations, community groups, and school personnel together to discuss educational issues as well as current concerns in the areas of health, recreation, defense, housing, food, and basic commodities.

Atlantic Coast—Bilingual Education: The devolution of decision-making power to regional offices of education is now occurring. This shift is most noticeable with regard to local responsibility for hiring and paying teachers and distributing educational materials. On the other hand, local level administrators are frequently reluctant to make important decisions or are incapable of doing so. Regional heads, selected by the Ministry of Education on the basis of lists submitted by ANDEN, are increasingly natives of the area. While this initially was not the case with heads of the Atlantic Coast special zones, this situation is changing.

The Atlantic Coast poses challenges to the central government concerning the proper balance between national integration and recognition of cultural and geographical differences, as well as the balance between the extractive and regulatory powers of central authorities, and the rights of local peoples to exercise some form of control over key areas of their lives. The indigenization of administrative and instructional personnel and the curriculum is found in attempts to establish bilingual education for the first four years of education.

Efforts to institute bilingual education were made during the Somoza period. In the 1950s, there was a pilot project in the Río Coco area to teach the Miskito inhabitants in their native tongue the first two years of basic education and to gradually introduce Spanish as a language of instruction. An external assessment of the project noted that the literacy project arrived "in the form of propaganda."[13] The young teachers who were sent to work in the project also were poorly prepared for the challenges they were to meet. The project failed to have any major or lasting effects on the area.

The tensions and tragedies that grip the Atlantic Coast region in the post-1979 period have been briefly discussed in Chapter 2 with reference to the 1980 and 1981 literacy campaigns. Despite charges of heavy-handed attempts to Hispanize the Atlantic Coast inhabitants, the campaign in native languages was a major step in the direction of more sensitive national approaches to cultural differences. Moreover, during the CNA, indigenous youth were used to teach Spanish and attempts were made to indigenize the curricula. Another significant move in the direction of greater cultural autonomy for the region was taken in December 1980, when the Sandinista government issued Decree 571. The decree recognizes that "the maternal language constitutes a fundamental factor in the existence of persons and peoples and is a determining factor in the process of integration and consolidation of National Unity." Article 1 thereby "authorizes instruction at the preprimary and in the first four grades of primary in the Miskito and English languages in the schools in the zone that said indigenous and Creole communities of the Atlantic Coast of Nicaragua occupy respectively." At the same time, the article states, instruction in the Spanish language shall be introduced in a gradual form.

As with the literacy campaign in indigenous language, the goal is not only instruction in the local tongues but the integration of these communities into the national political and economic systems.

An experimental project in bilingual education (grades one through four) was established in Sumubila in February 1984. A May 1984 Ministry of Education evaluation of the project noted the following problems, among others: inadequate preparation of teachers in political, pedagogical, and linguistic aspects of the project; insufficient priority assigned to the project by the ministry; failure to win support of the population of Sumubila; and selection of a Mestizo coordinator who did not speak Miskitu. Added to these difficulties were contra attacks, causing temporary dislocations of teachers and students, and the mobilization of the population to defend the area, thereby causing disruptions in instruction.[14] Further, the government was uncertain about the political loyalties of the surrounding communities. To remedy this situation, in part, a Miskito Indian, Mary Bushey Glasgow, was appointed to assume leadership of the project. Attempts also are being made to establish a preschool program in indigenous languages, which will be attached to the Normal School Pedro Aráuz Palacios in Puerto Cabezas, the major port city on the northeast coast and a militarily secure area.

Conceptually, it is not clear whether the bilingual program is a transitional one (with emphasis on preparing students to eventually use Spanish as the primary language of communication) or a maintenance one (preserving indigenous culture and language as the principal expression of ethnicity). The thrust appears to be on the transition to Spanish. Other issues include these: What texts will be used? To what extent will the pro-Sandinista content of the national curriculum be modified? Will methods of language instruction be changed to reflect the linguistic features of the indigenous languages?

With regard to the issue of texts, CIDCA (the Center for Investigation and Documentation of the Atlantic Coast) initiated in the fall of 1982 an innovative project to gather oral traditions of the Miskitos as the basis of instruction. (MED assumed responsibility for the project in May 1984.) Over 160 Miskito and Sumu oral traditions have been collected by a team of five researchers. In addition, a rich mine of oral traditions collected during the literacy campaign by the cultural brigades resides in the Ministry of Education's Museum of the National Literacy Crusade and in the Ministry of Culture.

Even with oral traditions serving as a basis for instruction, there is the question of the extent to which national content will infuse the curriculum. The pilot project not only calls for developing and vitalizing the values of "country," "national unity," "sovereignty," and "defense," but those of "anti-apartheid" and "proletarian internationalism," which, when compared with the pressing problem, for example, of defense, may not be of immediate concern to the inhabitants of the Atlantic Coast. Instead, they may be viewed as attempts to impose alien agendas and ideas on indigenous peoples.

The method of instruction also presents a thorny issue of linguistic significance. The Ministry of Education has introduced a "Phonic, Analytical, Synthetic Method" (FAS) to teach the Spanish language in the early grades. The method is suited to the phonetic and syntactical structures of Spanish, but not those of the indigenous and Creole languages of the Atlantic Coast. Planning documents indicate there is clear need for research on the linguistic, social, and cultural problems involved in an effective bilingual education program and the education programs that will build on the first four years of instruction. Funds, however, are scarce for research, as well as for the teacher preparation and bibliographical resources that will be needed to successfully implement the bilingual-bicultural program. The government has had to seek international financial assistance (approximately U.S. $35,000) to complete, for example, the oral traditions project. This lack of resources for education portends the larger difficulties of integrating the Atlantic Coast into national society. As noted in Chapter 2, without a greater sharing of resources between Pacific and Atlantic regions of the country, it is questionable whether even enlightened linguistic and cultural policies will have the desired effect.

Programs, Materials, and Methods

Prior to 1979, educational texts were acquired from abroad. The National Literacy Crusade, among other accomplishments, marked the first time that educational materials were designed and printed in Nicaragua. More than one million primers (literacy and mathematics texts) were published during the campaign. The follow-up adult basic education program (EPB) also has generated a demand for inexpensive print materials. During the first two years of its existence, 1981–83, four million texts were elaborated and published for free distribution.

During the Somoza period, texts were developed as part of the USAID-OAS project located in Guatemala City. U.S. text writers and curriculum specialists worked with teams from the various Central American republics on the elaboration of texts. Other major sources of texts were the Mexican affiliates of large U.S. publishing houses, which translated standard U.S. texts into Spanish. These books are still to be found in school libraries and are occasionally consulted for ideas in such areas as science and sex education. Generally, Nicaraguan curriculum developers and teachers, for nationalistic reasons and because of hostility to U.S. past and present interference in the internal affairs of their country, are reluctant to admit the value of these books or that they are used. Spanish texts, also found in school libraries, are in many respects as culturally inappropriate as those of North American publishers.

Other than the introductory reader, *Carlitos,* and national science texts (for grades three through five) developed as part of a special project (known as PERME) between the Federal Republic of Germany and the Nicaraguan government, students do not have texts—nor do teachers from primary through secondary education. Instead, they receive on a bimonthly basis study plans and program outlines, and methodological orientations. They meet one day every two months in workshops known as TEPCE (*Talleres de Evaluación, Programación y Capacticación Educativa*) to review the previous session's work and receive orientations for the next two months' curricular offerings. Primary school teachers are organized in the workshops by grade level (or in special groups for those who teach multigrade classrooms, typical of many rural schools); secondary education teachers meet according to subject matter specialization. (The TEPCEs will be discussed at greater length later in this chapter in the section on transformation in education.)

The Ministry of Education's Office of School Plans and Programs is in the process of developing permanent texts. In 1984, permanent texts were developed for grades 1 and 2. In 1985, grades 3, 5, and 7 were to be ready; in 1986, grades 4, 6, and 8; and in 1987, the last three years of secondary education (9–11). According to a first-hand report by David Myers, editor of *Mesoamerica,* these plans have been set back by the war situation in Nicaragua, with only the texts for the first two grades of primary being available in the spring of 1985.[15]

The introductory text, *Carlitos* (the name of the Sandinista young pioneer association), has undergone revisions and is now available in most schools. Where families have money, the text is purchased for 15 cordobas, or about 50 U.S. cents.

Carlitos merits discussion, as it reveals the pedagogical as well as ideological thrusts of the national government. The book starts with simple phonics lessons and illustrations of the flora and fauna of Nicaragua and scenes of everyday life. On page 48, the student is introduced to the FSLN and the content becomes increasingly related to symbols and images of importance to the FSLN. Among the recurrent themes is the role of youth in social change with specific reference to the Sandinista youth organizations, particularly ANS (*Asociación de Niños Sandinistas*). The young are the favorites of the revolution, but they also must study hard and prepare themselves to be useful to the country. Constant references are made throughout the text to national heroes Augusto César Sandino and Carlos Fonseca Amador, and to the importance of the Sandinista militias, army, and CDS in defending the country. The end section of the primer displays the Nicaraguan flag and the FSLN banner, contains the Nicaraguan and FSLN hymns, a poem by Rubén Darío, "*Del Trópico,*" and biographical portraits of Sandino and Fonseca. It also includes the story of the "Red Little Hen," with the moral that people have to work in order to eat.

In addition, the primer stresses the values of family and respect for nature. Many references are made to the Atlantic Coast region, its peoples and places of interest. The text occasionally mentions the efforts of the national government to initiate reforms to benefit the people of the region.

Carlitos 2, the follow-up text, begins with the statement, "We will tell you many things about other children, the family, the community, workers, plants, animals, our pretty country, Nicaragua, the revolution, and Great Men." The thematic content is essentially the same as the first volume of the primer. It is also interesting to note that honorific titles, such as *Don* and *Doña,* are used throughout the text, whereas in Cuba, these titles have all been abandoned for the more egalitarian *compañero.* Although the text calls for girls and boys to be good friends, respecting and helping each other (p. 26), occasionally sexist content appears as well as material that is extremely insensitive to disabled people. For example, there is a question concerning the uses of hands. The answers include, "to sweep and clean the patio as my mother does." In response to the question, "What would happen if you lost your hands?" there is the statement, "It would be horrible . . . because [I] could not learn to read and write—because with my hands I hold up the book to read and I use my hands to write." It is surprising that such a statement would pass scrutiny, particularly in a country where thousands have lost their limbs, first in the struggle to overthrow the Somoza regime, and subsequently in the battle against counterrevolutionary forces.

These points are mentioned not to denigrate the introductory readers, but to show that even with the most concerted of efforts to include progressive and pro-revolutionary content and images, contradictory and traditional material also finds its way into the texts. Secondly, even assuming that Nicaragua were unusual in including explicit political content in its readers, which is not the case (all countries attempt to use public school systems to indoctrinate the oncoming generation in the values of the national society), there is no guarantee that what is consciously and explicitly taught in school is what students learn. The effectiveness of instruction depends not only on content, but on the context and social relations of learning (themes which will be discussed later in this chapter).

With regard to pedagogy, the government also claims to have introduced an innovative teaching method that will improve the effectiveness of language instruction. FAS (*Fónico-Analítico-Sintético*) is a global method of language instruction that involves elements of phonics and whole word recognition. The following illustration of a basic lesson captures the different components involved.

a	e	o
ma	me	mo
mama	memo	amo

Mama me amo

[Primer includes a photograph of a mother and child.]

In a lesson, students may learn to pronounce individual letters, sylla-bles, whole words, and whole sentences. Given basic words as building blocks, they are encouraged to construct their own sentences.

The method is new to Nicaraguan educators and confusing to many parents. Teachers receive 15 days' training in the method, which accord-ing to a number of teachers is not an adequate period to cover such topics as how to work with individual students. As utilized by an experienced and competent teacher—which is often not the case—the method appears to work well, and students progress rapidly in learning to pronounce and sight read whole sentences. But even with well prepared teachers, there are problems. The method depends on children working with packets of letters and syllables to construct words and sentences. These materials frequently do not arrive on time; and then distribution is so time-consum-ing in large classes that classroom order may degenerate. Even the phonetically regular Spanish language may pose some problems, as, for example, with the letters "b" and "v," which are pronounced the same. Some parents have indicated that without their support, the students have difficulty in catching on and doing well with the method. Another prob-lem is that students read print letters, but by grade three are expected to write in cursive.

The FAS work book complements *Carlitos* pedagogically and politi-cally. The sentences that are constructed with the linguistic building blocks refer not only to the family but also, for example, to the importance of manual work and the need to recognize and reward the laboring groups in the society.

The political and social themes that are introduced in these begin-ning readers are found throughout the curriculum at higher levels. In the math texts, as in adult education, exercises frequently contain socially rel-evant messages such as this: In a health center there are 13 nurses and seven doctors. How many health persons staff the Health Center? By comparison, math exercises in the United States might involve how many consumer items can be purchased by a boy or girl who had saved a certain amount of money.

The only area of the curriculum in which political content is expressly curtailed is that of the natural sciences, grades three through five. Since

1981, over 2.4 million inexpensive science texts have been published as part of the PERME project (*Proyecto de Elaboración y Reproducción de Materiales Educativos*) with the West German government. The technical assistance between the two countries prohibits the introduction of explicit political subject matter. Initially, the project involved development of texts in places such as Estelí and Jinotega, with regional variation in content. Then, each regional center became responsible for the publication of a single national text for different grade levels—for example, Jinotega was responsible for fourth grade science. As of late 1984, the design and development of texts was centralized in Managua.

The project has been enormously successful as well as significant in its educational implications. The wide-scale printing and dissemination of the PERME texts means that most children in upper grades of primary education have a free text with which to study. Also, the materials call for independent as well as group work, and make frequent suggestions for activities and experiments that will enable students to gain a practical appreciation of science. When outside guests visit Nicaraguan schools, it is probable that they are shown a natural science class or session, because it is most commonly the part of the curriculum that works best—thanks to the PERME materials.

This is not to imply that there are not problems with the PERME materials. The fourth grade text developed by the regional center in Jinotega often confused teachers with poorly designed experiments. What is encouraging is that the regional team of teachers who devised the text received feedback and in the spring of 1984 openly criticized their own mistakes as well as some of the national guidelines which, they said, did not reflect many of the constraints on teachers in their region (it being a war zone), and which were probably more appropriate for urban school children.

If some teachers might be charged as "counterrevolutionaries" for criticizing the national curriculum, such fears did not deter the group in Jinotega who lambasted what they considered to be inappropriate directives and content emanating from Managua.

Public critiques of education center not only on the political content of instruction but also on academic standards. Those unfavorable to the revolution remark that during the Somoza years, children were expected to know much more than they are presently learning. One reason is that much of the curriculum, according to them, is devoted to political indoctrination. Those favorable to the revolution might point out the elitist nature of the previous system and that it also was no less doctrinaire than the present curriculum, the difference being in what values were emphasized.

Few would criticize the curriculum as being too academic. Yet, a disinterested examination of the curriculum might indicate that this is indeed the case. To take the example of the first year mathematics curriculum for the diversified cycle of secondary education (grade ten), the unit on real variable functions is good, according to one Latin American math educator,[16] but it is also very formal mathematically. She questions the usefulness of this type of mathematics to the majority, especially those who will not pursue further education. The unit, and possibly much of the secondary school mathematics curriculum, may be primarily geared to the small proportion of high school students who will go on to college. The topic, nonetheless, does have potential relevance to everyday problems of significance to the country. For example, the unit could include the reading and interpretation of graphs from newspapers and magazines. These activities, according to the math educator, would provide an informal introduction to the concept, stressing its applicability, before going into the formal study of the concept.

This example illustrates a general concern on the part of a number of Nicaraguan policy makers (particularly those concerned with the economic consequences of schooling) that the education system, as presently constituted, is too disarticulated from the country's immediate problems. While the content of texts and curriculum programs are undergoing revision to accord with the social and political transformations occurring in the country, the overall thrust of postprimary education remains essentially academic and university preparatory. Despite the plaque outside the MED office (in the spring of 1984) which read "Middle School Education," postprimary education is no longer defined as such; since 1983, it has been designated as "secondary" education. Of the 13,887 graduates from the intermediate level of education in that year, 8,380 were enrolled in the academic branch; fewer than 500 were in agricultural and industrial education; 3,208 were in commercial studies; and 1,720 in teacher training normal schools.

There have been efforts to "technify" secondary education by placing more emphasis on the sciences (physics, chemistry, and biology). But many students continue to prefer to study the humanities. In the words of the director of secondary education, in 1984, Nicaragua "still did not have an appropriate revolutionary education."[17] At this level, efforts to transform secondary education and relate it more to the economic development goals of the country have included academic olympics, a special association of honors students (*Liga de Saber*), and national science fairs. With the exception of the latter (which will be discussed in greater detail in the subsequent section), these innovations tend to reinforce elitist, scholastic aspects of secondary education—a tendency which is difficult to avoid in a society emphasizing the need for rapid technological and scientific development.

Technical Education

The most nebulous area of postprimary education is technical education. Despite the significance of this area to economic growth, and to socialist notions of "polyvalent education" (an education that combines productive labor with academic studies, recreational activities, political socialization, cultural awareness and expression), technical education is poorly conceptualized, enrolls few students, and is costly and heavily dependent on external credit lines from friendly countries, particularly those of the Eastern bloc. From the viewpoint of planning, technical education has been characterized by disorganized growth and fragmented effort between the public and private sectors, and within the public sector between the MED, CNES (National Higher Education Council), different ministries, and SINAFORP. There has been debate over how many levels and types of technical degrees should be offered—presently three at the preuniversity level[18]—and to what extent basic education itself should include general vocational orientation and special skill training. The following brief review of the different types of technical education illustrates major issues as well as attempts to address them.

Agricultural education (*Educación Técnica Agropecuaria*) consists of a variety of programs, none of which reaches large numbers of students. Enrollment in postprimary technical agricultural schools has grown substantially from only 580 students in 1980. But still, as of 1984, it was little more than 3,000 in a country where development is critically related to modernizing the agricultural sector.

Industrial education now reaches close to 5,000 students, with the electrical and mechanical branches being the most popular. The cost per pupil still is very high, given large capital outlays for new physical plant. The director of the La Salle Technical Institute of León estimates, for example, that the yearly costs of a student in his technical school are approximately 11,000 cordobas, compared with approximately 1,500 cordobas for a secondary school student.

On the positive side, wage policies of the government are sufficiently attractive to recruit greater numbers of students to technical fields and guarantee that many will be motivated to enter the work force upon graduation, rather than set their sights on further studies at the university level. A middle-level technician (TM) with the equivalent of a high school degree within five years of graduating can earn approximately the same monthly pay as a university graduate in a high demand area (7,000 to 8,000 cordobas). (An engineer working for the state might earn a top salary of 9,000 to 10,000 cordobas.) However, as the course requirements for a TM (*Técnico Medio*) are essentially the same as those of a high school graduate (*Bachillerato*), there still may be an inducement to substantial numbers of students to pursue a prestigious university degree.

By far the largest number of vocationally-oriented students continue to enroll in commercial education. Fifty percent of these students are studying in private schools, which, for the most part, receive state subsidies or assistance. Although the state is now controlling the abuses that existed prior to 1979 when commercial education was largely a profit-making enterprise, to speak of quality education in these schools, according to the head of commercial education, "would be romantic."[19]

For the most part, commercial education turns out clericals and accountants. In 1985, however, it began to offer new courses at the TM level in statistics and planning. Rather than state the expected salary graduates would earn (approximately 4,000–5,000 cordobas), mass media advertisements announced that "a new career was being opened in accordance with the necessities of the country." Within eight days, 150–170 candidates had responded to the public announcement—90 percent of them male.

Trends in women's enrollment in technical education programs is a subject worthy of analysis. Are females being recruited to nontraditional technical careers, or are they concentrated in education programs that will prepare them for traditional roles? Females account for approximately 25 percent of students enrolled in agricultural-technical education. In the industrial fields, they tend to be concentrated in food, textiles, and architectural design; in commercial studies, in clerical occupations. Women also represent the overwhelming majority of students in normal schools, which have the responsibility for training primary school teachers.

Teachers

Central to upgrading the quality of the education system are efforts to improve the preparation, inservice training, and working conditions of teachers. In 1983, 8,900 teachers at the primary and secondary levels were without the requisite training. Uncertified teachers account for approximately one-half (51 percent) of teachers (excluding higher education and adult education). The planning office of MED estimates that teacher training institutions will have to nearly triple their first year enrollments per annum between 1985 and 1990 in order to meet current demands.[20]

Attracting talented youth to the teaching profession and retaining superior teachers have presented major challenges to MED. In the early months of 1984 alone, 2,000 primary school teachers renounced the profession due primarily to difficult working conditions and extremely poor remuneration (2,000 to 2,500 cordobas per month). Because of the operations of a free market, teachers were able to leave MED for other ministries, such as health, and immediately to begin earning 1,000 cordobas more a month. Many ambitious teachers also sought supervisory positions within MED with the possibility of nearly doubling their salaries. On June 14, 1984, the Ministry of Education made an historic announcement: for the first time in the country's history, teachers would be paid salaries equivalent to those of comparable professionals. The salary agreement reached between ANDEN and MED increased the salaries of certified primary school teachers from 2,000 to 4,000 cordobas a month; and for uncertified teachers (*maestros empíricos*) from 1,800 to 3,500. Certified secondary school teachers enjoyed a monthly raise from 4,000 to 7,500 cordobas, while uncertified teachers were to receive as much as 6,500. The decision to increase teacher compensation was taken in accordance with revisions already underway in the mining and manufacturing sectors of the economy—known by the rather unusual acronym of SNOT (*Sistema Nacional del Organización de Trabajo,* National System for the Organization of Work).

Other steps taken in 1983–84 to improve working conditions consisted of placing a limit of 25 hours on the academic load of primary school teachers and reducing the weekly number of hours of secondary school teachers from 40 to 34, and of normal school teachers to 30. Because of the poor pay of teachers in the past, however, many teachers took advantage of these reduced loads to teach two sessions or to pick up extra subjects and classes outside their normal schedules.

Attracting and retaining large numbers of teachers does not guarantee that they will be academically and pedagogically competent nor, in the eyes of the Sandinista leadership, politically correct. In addition to the expansion of normal schools from five to 14, and the institution of "distance education" to prepare teachers by means of correspondence materials and intensive weekend sessions, a further source of teachers is the Sandinista Youth Organization (JS–19 J). In 1983–84, 1,600 secondary school students were sent to Cuba to be trained as teachers in an intensive one-year course. Members of this special brigade, bearing the name, "Fiftieth Anniversary of the Death of Sandino," were to serve anywhere in the country for a period of two years. There is also a one-year period of obligatory social service for graduates of teacher training institutions, who usually are sent to rural areas.

The decision makers concerned with the political correctness of teachers believe that future teachers will increasingly have to be selected from among secondary school graduates who are politically militant. Such recruits would then receive intensive training in pedagogy and the foundations of education. Whether sufficient youth of this political stripe can be recruited into teaching is problematic, given competing demands on them from other priority areas—military service, to name one. Moreover, there is a tremendous need for talented youth to enter technical and scientific fields. At best, the proposal represents a temporary measure, relieving shortages created not only by past deficits and large-scale exodus from the profession, but by the efforts of the government to replace the 1,500 Cuban teachers who comprise the Pedagogical Contingent, "Augusto César Sandino." The proposal, in 1984, further reflected the desire of Nicaragua not to be overly dependent on any country, even a friendly one such as Cuba, and also the efforts of the Sandinista government to dissipate U.S. concern over a Cuban "presence."

The burden of preparing, and even reshaping, a qualitatively different teaching force necessarily rests on preservice and inservice programs. It would appear that normal schools may have changed the content of instruction to better reflect what the Sandinistas consider worthy of learning by future teachers, but not the processes of acquiring and utilizing knowledge. As will be noted in the subsequent section, transformations in education depend upon transformations in the ways in which teachers relate to students, and students to one another. Much of the instruction in normal schools appears to follow the traditional, didactic method and involves little inquiry on the part of students. The shortages of basic learning materials, occasioned by the war situation, partially account for these problems, but so do the lack of qualified teachers and the dependence of the country on outside teachers who themselves may be quite traditional in their pedagogical philosophy and methods.

The inservice programs and modalities established by MED offer perhaps the most promising route to follow in upgrading and transforming the teaching force. Among the most exciting innovations are the TEPCEs. The "workshops" started as monthly meetings of teachers to evaluate the past month's activities and to discuss the next set of teacher guides and curriculum materials. They were conceived as teacher collectives that would constantly be criticizing, formulating, and reformulating an appropriate education according to changing circumstances in the country. Over time, however, the TEPCEs have evolved into bimonthly meetings that have lost much of their grassroots character, with directives and programs being passed down from the ministry through the regional and district bureaucracies to teachers at the bottom end. While the transformative aspect may have diminished in the process, there is also no question that MED has done a remarkable job through the TEPCEs and vacation-time courses of offering numerous and systematic opportunities for teachers to improve their knowledge and skills.

At the regional-level pre-TEPCEs, the hierarchy of MED and ANDEN hash out new policies and the strategies for implementing them. At the June 1984 regional pre-TEPCE in the Normal School of San Marcos, outside Managua, I witnessed a discussion on how to inculcate in the youth of the country the value of respect for social property and a more scientific-materialistic view of the world. Inevitably, the national- and regional-level MED administrators and school principals turned to the need for changes in teachers themselves. At times, the meeting bore a slight resemblance to a religious revival, with the educators denouncing their own failings and reaffirming their commitment to the revolution. While the creation of a new education system—and in the process, possibly a new Nicaraguan person—is linked to an expanded and improved teaching force, it is also very much dependent on transformations in the social relations of learning and in the relations between schooling, community, and economy.

TRANSFORMATIONS

As noted earlier in the chapter, transformations in education are linked by MED ideologues and planners to a new model of economic accumulation. This model is based on state control over strategic levers of the economy (banking, foreign commerce, pricing and distribution of basic commodities), on an expanded sector of public ownership, and on workers playing a more significant role in decision making at the plant level and through central labor unions at the national level. Sandinista goals for the agricultural sector envision various types of cooperatives playing a major role in production, with the large state agro-industrial enterprising accounting for about 20 percent of output. In general, the development of the economy is to be guided by the "logic of the majority."

According to the middle-range plan of MED, "Education has a different ideology because it has another meaning, to prepare a new work force at the service of new relations of production."[21] Education is expected to overcome the gaps that traditionally exist between theory and practice, intellectual and manual work, schooling and community. The new person that emerges from this system is to be altruistic, cooperative, participatory, and self-abnegating for the collective good. Education is to be "insurrectional, popular, political, democratic, participatory, permanent, associated with work, scientific and humanistic."[22] The formation of a "new person" is predicated upon the assumption that the social relations of learning are undergoing change in revolutionary Nicaragua, as are the relations between school, workplace, and community.

Social Relations of Learning

The social relations of learning refer to whether or not teaching-learning situations are authoritarian or democratic, competitive or cooperative, alienating or integrating.[23] These relations comprise a hidden curriculum of expectations and incentives for behavior that shape norms and general value orientations.[24]

From kindergarten on, there is an attempt to emphasize a more cooperative and collectively oriented disposition on the part of youth. At the same time, the norms of independence and individual achievement[25] are also encouraged at all levels. In kindergarten, for example, children share crayons, scissors, and other school materials, but they also are expected to perform on their own. The most noticeable changes in student learning and work patterns occur in the upper grades of primary and continue on through university studies. As in Cuba and in the USSR, students form study circles of approximately five to ten students, and they select a monitor themselves. The monitors, usually academically superior students, are expected to assist the others with their studies.[26] A number of classroom assignments involve group efforts, and a certain percentage of the student's grade will reflect group performance. Usually, however, the major examinations require individual, unabetted performance, and the greatest percentage of the student's final grades will be based on each student's own achievement.

Generally, in Nicaragua as elsewhere, the use of study groups as a pedagogically valuable device is based on the premise that a group's knowledge is greater than that of any single individual, that group learning will tend to raise the level of knowledge of the academically weakest members of a group, that the social values of cooperation and collective approaches to problem solving are enhanced, and that the student peer groups become a strong aid in encouraging prosocial behavior and in controlling antisocial behavior. This reliance on student groups to encourage achievement orientation and desired socialization outcomes contrasts strikingly with widespread negative views of peer, especially adolescent, subcultures in the United States.[27]

The difficulties with heavy reliance on study groups is that an effective methodology has yet to be evolved that would facilitate group learning. What often occurs is that individuals arrive at group study sessions unprepared, expecting the group to resolve problems. This seldom happens. Group work is no substitute for individual effort and study prior to coming together with others.[28] What may result is shared ignorance.

Group learning is also evident in the classroom. Frequently, students are formed into circles to discuss topics or solve problems. The PERME natural science texts commonly call for group discussion.

These patterns of home study and classroom learning depart significantly from the more competitive and individualistic/atomized approaches characteristic of education systems throughout Latin America. In Nicaragua, the domination of classroom transactions and one-way flow of information from teacher to students is diminished to a certain extent by these more group-oriented activities and emphases. It would be incorrect, however, to assume that classroom learning relations may now be characterized as democratic and inquiry-oriented with students playing a more active role in the determination of the objectives, content, methods, and pacing of instruction.

The Nicaraguan classroom is still very much teacher-dominated and, for the most part, characterized by a didactic, scholastic approach to learning. This situation is a reflection not only of the persistence of old pedagogical patterns and the low level of training of most teachers, but also of the poverty of the country.

The government has made extraordinary efforts to distribute texts to all school children, particular in the first two grades of primary education. The number of school libraries was planned to grow to 360 by 1984, and science laboratories and workshops were to be installed in schools. Despite these efforts, there is still a widespread paucity of learning materials. Most libraries contain few books, and laboratories and workshops are characterized by bare bones conditions. The physical destruction wreaked by the *contra* attacks and the difficulty of distributing materials to schools in war zones were noted in previous sections.

The main source of information, in most cases, remains the teacher, with student notes of teacher dictations serving as the primary text. In many respects, therefore, the school system remains hierarchical; and the school ladder, with each rung leading up to the coveted goal of a university education, is unchanged. Old prestige patterns are well entrenched whereby university graduates wish to be called "doctor" or "engineer" and command greater deference than ordinary laborers. It is these old patterns that the new education system is attempting to address through its efforts to link schooling more directly to the world of work.

Relations to Work

From kindergarten on, emphasis is placed on teaching students notions concerning the dignity of work, and that it is through work that people transform the world and in the process become human. According to teacher guidelines elaborated in the spring of 1984 for primary school teachers,[29] "One of the conditions most important for the realization of the tasks of education in a new society is to link study with productive and socially useful labor." Among the examples of socially useful labor that students must perform are helping to repair school equipment, working in school gardens, and cleaning the schools.

In line with these curricular emphases, two to three hours a week are set aside in upper primary education for vocational study. MED has established approximately 100 multipurpose workshops serving clusters of schools. Students may study wood working, electricity, sewing, and cooking. In addition, a number of urban schools and most rural schools cultivate vegetable gardens. The ministry, through its Program of Communal Educational Development (PRODECO), provides gardening tools and technical assistance to schools setting up garden plots.

The scope and impact of the above efforts, however, are presently limited. As noted earlier, most primary school workshops are poorly equipped; not all schools participate in the workshop program; the amount of time involved in manual work is minimal; and even in rural areas, where there is an abundance of land, most garden plots are very small and insufficiently cultivated to produce enough food for a school lunch program.

More ambitious programs include Peasant Agricultural Schools (*Escuelas Agropecuarias Campesinas*—EACs) that offer the equivalent of a sixth grade education and specific skill training, and Rural Work-Study Schools (*Escuelas Rurales de Educación Trabajo*—ERETs). In 1984, there were only four EACs and ten ERETs, but the government planned to open two more ERETs late in the year. There also were seven CBPs (*Ciclos Básicos de Producción*), rural junior high schools (grades seven through nine) that emphasize agricultural studies in combination with the academic curriculum.

Nicaragua, in contrast to Cuba, is only in the beginning stages of establishing work-study programs that reach most students and accomplish the twin goals of instilling an appreciation of manual (especially agricultural) labor while also generating needed resources and income. Since 1971, Cuba has constructed nearly 600 rural schools for secondary education students (grades seven through nine) that appear to be successful on both accounts.

One last problem is sex role stereotyping in determining the appropriateness of certain types of work. In the primary school workshop program, boys invariably gravitate toward carpentry and electronics, the girls toward sewing and cooking. In a number of schools, a lottery has been instituted to achieve a more equitable distribution of boys and girls among the different workshops. Not unexpectedly, parents have protested their sons being assigned to sewing and cooking classes. School personnel have argued that boys who may be drafted need to have these skills, and this argument carries some weight with parents. But they still object to their sons doing "female" work like sewing.

Despite these shortcomings and limitations, there are a number of programs and activities that do appear to be effective. Schools, particularly at the upper primary and secondary levels, encourage their students to be involved in community service and may give academic credit for it. As noted in Chapter 2, thousands of youth have been involved in various agricultural harvests, going to work for one to two months during vacation periods. Schools arrange special make-up sessions and examinations for students who fall behind in their academic work due to their involvement in these production mobilizations, which are vital to the economic well being of the country.

In addition to their direct involvement in these national projects, students are encouraged to contribute their talents and energies to the study and possible resolution of technical and scientific problems confronting the country. In technical institutes, such as La Salle in León, the emphasis is on teaching students to design machines and undertake projects that lead to socially useful products and services.

By far the most extensive and promising project which links education to work is that of the national science fairs (*Jornadas Estudiantiles de Ciencia y Producción*). Initiated in 1981 by the Sandinist Youth Organization, MED, and ANDEN, the fairs annually involve more than 15,000 high school students, close to 1,000 teachers, and over 2,000 projects. Students form work groups, find sponsoring teachers and technical advisors from the community, consult with state agencies and mass organizations on worthwhile projects, and design and execute projects in the areas of infrastructure, industry, technology, agriculture, conservation of natural resources, health, and education. By way of illustration, I will describe projects from two schools I visited.

Two students at the La Salle Technical Institute of León, Byron William Sumariba and Marta Rodríguez, worked one to two hours daily over a six-month period under the guidance of a visiting Austrian teacher to design alternative energy sources for rural populations. In their words, they "took into account the needs of peasants" and suggested ways of converting wind energy into electrical energy. Their project won a regional prize in the area of infrastructure. They are now working on electrical circuit models to facilitate teaching of electronics. Although they are both of working class backgrounds, they plan to study engineering abroad.

At the Rural Educational Núcleo (NER) of Rama, a group of nighttime students, including a farmer in his thirties, developed a variety of uses for ginger. The older student had worked in a cooperative that cultivated 150 *manzanas* of ginger. The students estimated that the cooperative had lost nearly U.S. $1 million due to difficulties in storing, processing, and marketing (nationally and internationally) the crop. The group first reviewed the history of the farm, which had been owned by a U.S. businessman, and pointed out the implications of foreign control over marketing and pricing of the commodity, and the problems that resulted when the farm was converted to a cooperative after the 1979 revolution. The students, in a very simple school science laboratory, invented an amazing variety of food and medical products: tea, biscuits, condiments, soft drinks and alcoholic beverages, a digestive aid, cough syrup, and an antipiretic. The project won a national prize. In addition, another group in the Rama high school (the base school for a NER) won a similar prize for designing ways of constructing houses with fortified adobe. Although few entries in the local and national science competitions are of the quality of these projects, they indicate the contributions that students can make to the nation.

Extraordinary significance is accorded to the national exhibition of science fair projects held in Managua. The inauguration of the fair in the last week of October 1984 was attended by the Minister of Education and over half a dozen other ministers and heads of national corporations. In the final week of the national electoral campaign, junta member and Sandinista vice-presidential candidate, Sergio Ramírez Mercado, handed out the awards to the national finalists. The significance of these fairs, as articulated by Minister of Education Fernando Cardenal, was this: the progress of Nicaragua depended on the development of the critical, scientific, and creative talents of its youth; and these fairs were an example of the government's commitment to fostering these talents.

Finalists of the national science competitions in high schools are placed in contact with winners from a parallel competition occurring in industry. As organized by the Sandinista Labor Central (CST), the Ministry of Labor, MIPLAN, and other state entities, the competition encourages innovations in the workplace. An examination of the sample of workers participating in the 1983 competition from the region of Managua indicates that almost 90 percent had less than a secondary school degree and one finalist did not even have a primary school degree. One of the projects that won a national prize consisted of operations to repair a German thermal turbine in Nicaragua. Previously, the machine had to be taken out of production for three months or more to be sent to Germany to be repaired at more than ten times the cost of fixing it at home.

School-Community Relations

Perhaps the most innovative aspects of the formal education system during the past five years of Sandinista rule are found in attempts to integrate schooling with community and national life. Among notable efforts to do so were 1) a massive national consultation, in early 1981, of public opinion concerning various aspects of the pre- and post-1979 education systems, and 2) the establishment of rural education *núcleos* (NERs) to serve as the infrastructure for community involvement in the resolution of pressing problems.

The national consultation was an unprecedented effort to elicit large-scale input into the shaping of the new education system. Over a two-month period (January and February 1981), 50,000 Nicaraguans participated in the discussion of a 55-item questionnaire concerning the outcomes and shortcomings of the pre-1979 education system, and the "Goals, Objectives, and Principles of the New Education System."

Discussions at the municipal level were summarized by 30 mass and private organizations at the departmental and national levels. The largest number (20,797) participated in the consultation through the mechanisms of the Sandinista Defense Committees (CDS). Surprisingly, the second largest number of participants (7,498) belonged to MISURASATA (which in 1981 joined the counterrevolutionary forces attempting to topple the Sandinista government),[30] the Sandinista Youth (2,549), AMNLAE (2,082), and ANDEN (1,611). In terms of greatest geographic coverage, the CDS, ANDEN, and JS–19 J consulted their membership in 106, 100, and 87 municipalities respectively. Although most major educational, syndical, professional, and religious groups participated in the national consultation, several major political parties and one radical labor union did not. These include the Popular Social Christian Party (PPSC), the Democratic Conservative Party (PCD), the Social Christian Party (PSC), and the Confederation of Labor Unification (CUS). Several important business groups, such as the Confederation of Chambers of Commerce (CCC) participated only in the initial training phase of the project, and the Chamber of Nicaraguan Industry (CADIN) submitted its report to the opposition newspaper *La Prensa* rather than send it through normal channels.[31] With the exception of CADIN, the summaries of the consultation went to the National Educational Advisory Council, the government junta, and the FSLN National Directorate.

The summaries indicate general concern with, for example, the eradication of illiteracy, the institutionalization of free universal education, and the extension of basic education services to the Atlantic Coast; and they illustrate current notions of such concepts as popular democracy in contemporary Nicaragua. Eighteen of the 30 organizations defined popular democracy as "the active participation of the organized people in executive, legislative and judicial actions of the government, as well as participation in the tasks and achievements of the Revolution in the political-social and in the economic-cultural [areas]. This was the most common definition, followed by 10 organizations listing as a central attribute of popular democracy the "enjoyment of individual rights without fear of being repressed."[32]

The summaries provide general statements that only with great difficulty could serve as the basis for policy. For example, with regard to the ideal qualities of the new Nicaraguan person, the national consultation highlighted these characteristics: in the political realm, the qualities of "patriotism, social solidarity, internationalism, social engagement and [respect for] national unity"; in the social or interpersonal realm, "discipline, cooperation, responsibility, creativity, efficiency, cooperation and hard work"; in the personal domain, "respectfulness, humanism, truthfulness, sincerity, and honesty."[33]

The significance of the national consultation is best summarized by the MED:

> The National Consultation signified an extraordinary experience in self-education for the participating organizations. For the grand majority of them, it was the first time that they had the possibility of freely discussing questions traditionally considered to be technical and therefore beyond the opinion of majority sectors of the population.[34]

There are two other examples of widescale solicitation of student as well as community input into educational processes. One occurred during the first month of schooling after the July 1979 victory of the Sandinistas, and the other is the use of the *De Cara al Pueblo* format by Minister of Education Fernando Cardenal. The first month of classes, in effect, consisted of a national dialogue in which students were encouraged to discuss the war against the Somoza regime, their fears and concerns. The former minister of education, Carlos Tünnermann Bernheim, has described the process as a type of catharsis for many youth who were traumatized by the 1977–79 period, in which thousands of youths were combatants against, as well as victims of, the National Guard.[35]

A more recent device for student and community input, initiated in 1984, consists of the Minister of Education and other MED functionaries visiting schools and education centers throughout the country and addressing issues and concerns raised by the audience—very much in the same manner that members of the national government respond to community questions on the televised program, *De Cara al Pueblo*. There are indications, however, that the pace of the consultations was slowed down in 1985, due to the war situation in the country.

The NERs represent the most extensive vehicle for rural areas to participate in the identification and resolution of a broad range of school and community concerns. Administratively, NERs are an old idea—predating the Sandinista regime and utilized in a number of Latin American countries, notably the Andean countries of Colombia, Peru, and Bolivia.

The rural *núcleo* concept, described earlier in this chapter with regard to trends in centralization-decentralization, provides an organizational means of sharing scarce resources among dispersed schools and overcoming their isolation. What is unusual about the NERs, in the case of Nicaragua, is not only the care with which the NERs are designed to reach as large a population as possible,[36] but their close tie-in with community development. The concept of popular participation involves school-community councils, with representatives of relevant state entities and mass organizations, discussing problems in the areas of social services, defense, and production.[37] Problems first identified at the grassroots level of the satellite schools are then progressively discussed at the sub-base and base levels. Tremendous emphasis is placed on preparing rural working-class people to gain the skills and self-confidence to identify and resolve everyday problems through community action. In many respects, this is classic community development work.

In the spring of 1984, only a few NERs had operational school-community councils, and these were in the incipient stages of development. The base-level assembly I attended in Villa Carlos Fonseca in mid-June illustrated both the promise and reality of grassroots democracy. The satellite and sub-base representatives, who had previously discussed community concerns, were, for a variety of reasons, unable to attend the more general assembly. Alternate delegates who arrived did not feel competent to chair the group discussions or serve as rapporteurs. Representatives of state agencies also were not well versed in procedures for conducting the meetings and at times tended to dominate. But the assembly organizers from the NER base school and the MED Office of Rural Nuclearization circulated among the groups, patiently explaining the philosophy of the assemblies and the procedures for conducting the meetings along more participatory lines. By the end of the day, most of the community people were assuming responsibility for chairing the meetings, no matter how imperfectly; and the various work groups had identified selected problems and concrete steps that could be taken over the coming weeks to do something about them.

The desire to produce results by the end of three or four hours of group discussion and have a report to be circulated among the various schools of a NER, however, may have conflicted with the educational goal of participants learning the skills of running their own meetings and identifying their own problems and the steps they could take to resolve them. Throughout the assembly there was a tension between process and product emphases, between the equally laudable aims of encouraging community participation in decision making and actually getting things done.

Despite these problems, the NERs represent one of the more exciting reforms occurring within the education system. The NERs link school to society. Although some critics object to schools serving as the vehicle for community development in rural areas, the NER networks do provide one of the few existing mechanisms for bringing diverse groups together and tackling problems along a broad front, as well as in the more specific area of education. In addition, popular participation represents a means of extending education and also emphasizing the value of social solidarity and communal action.

The Ministry of Education, cognizant of this situation, is conducting detailed studies through its Office of Rural Nuclearization of human resources, political leadership, and economic resources to suggest ways in which popular participation can contribute to rural development. Grassroots participation represents an important means of maintaining rural infrastructure and, more specifically, lowering the costs of school construction by approximately one-half. Community volunteer labor accounts for a majority of the 1,404 schools built in the countryside since 1979. According to MED specialists in rural school construction, a school built with community participation may cost as little as 60,000 cordobas and be more attractive and suitable for Nicaragua's tropical climate than a school built by a private firm using funds from a World Bank sector loan. In the latter case, costs may be as high as 180,000 cordobas.[38]

Transformations in School Culture

In addition to changes in the social relations of learning, and the relations between schooling and society, there have been transformations in the material culture of schools, in the range and types of extra- or co-curricular activities that comprise much of the life of schools. The classroom walls, school corridors, and bulletin boards systematically bombard students and teachers with the images of national heroes (Sandino, Fonseca, and other FSLN founders) and local martyrs. Banners and posters exhort them to participate in defense activities and production brigades, to work hard and conserve natural resources. In the month of May, extraordinary attention was accorded to Mothers' Day, and to the sacrifices of mothers whose children had been mobilized to fight the counterrevolutionaries.

MED places great emphasis on the correct display of symbols related to national heroes and martyrs. Two MED supervisors (who accompanied me on a school visit) were especially critical in their site report to the principal of a fourth grade teacher's exhibit of the life of Sandino: they said it was confusing and that it was too important a subject to display poorly.

Similar importance is attached to the flag raising and lowering ceremonies, on Monday morning and Friday afternoon respectively. On these occasions, members of the ANS or JS–19 J give a talk to the assembled students on themes such as the life of one of the FSLN martyred founders or on the aggression the country is facing. It is difficult for outsiders to invest these ceremonies with the same degree of solemnity and emotion accorded them by Sandinista militants or sympathizers. These events have profound significance for those people who were involved in the struggle to topple the Somoza regime and for those who are presently defending the country against external aggression and internal sabotage. The flag and symbols of the fallen combatants are equated with great suffering and loss of loved ones as well as, in the words of the Sandinista hymn, the dawn of a new order which offers greater justice for all.

Not all is solemn and subdued. There is also an air of festivity that surrounds the activities of the JS–19 J and the Federation of Secondary Students (FES), which, as of 1984, was the mass organization of high school students. (In the meantime, the JS–19 J, as well as ANS, has become a vanguard political organization of the FSLN reporting directly to Bayardo Arce, political coordinator of the FSLN National Directorate.) The JS–19 J and FES are constantly organizing activities: inviting students to dances, to fund raisers for the militias, reserves, and production brigades; and urging students to participate in Patriotic Military Service (the draft).

The efficacy of these constant exhortations and mobilizations, symbolic rituals and displays is difficult to ascertain. In many schools, the images are mixed—traditional images of the mother and the teacher are fused with new role expectations and different ways of viewing these figures; depictions of the life of workers and peasants coexist with those of middle-class suburban families (clipped from magazines glorifying cosmopolitan life in the United States or Western Europe); national folk figures are pasted on school walls alongside Walt Disney characters. Inspirational messages delivered in student assemblies compete with the boredom and tedium of standing too long and listening to barely comprehensible speakers droning on. National anthem, FSLN hymn, Christian prayer, and school song may follow one another in what seems to be a natural sequence. Sandinista youth organizations celebrate the joys of youth and life in post-1979 Nicaragua along with the sacrifices the young are called upon to shoulder, if there is to be a tomorrow.

No matter how confusing this melange of images and messages may be—and this is typical of Nicaragua, as well as any society in the initial stages of a revolution—it is also certain that the ethos of youth culture has changed. Expectations, even in the most elitist private institutions, also have changed markedly over the past five years.

Youths who volunteer for military service are a source of pride in schools such as the Jesuit-founded Colegio Centroamérica, once a bastion of the elite[39] but which has, since 1980, experienced significant change in the social class composition of its student body. In the center of its plush campus, there is a plaque commemorating 22 students who had "offered their lives in the struggle for liberation." As one of the fifth-year student leaders noted, "Being in a high school with a religious orientation, we understand that you ought to participate more belligerently in the defense of revolutionary power."[40] By June 1984, 130 students had volunteered for military service and 120 had signed up to participate in the upcoming November coffee harvest. The JS–19 J is not the only youth organization at the school; some 50 students belonged to Christian Students for the

Revolution, which had the goal of integrating the "largest number of Christian students into the tasks of the revolution."[41] The changes in more traditional schools, like Centroamérica, are indicative of transformations throughout the education system. There may not be a totally different Nicaraguan youth, but there are more opportunities, as well as increased expectations, to act in new and more socially conscious ways.

SUMMARY

Since 1979, there has been a marked expansion of primary and secondary education. In its wake, this expansion has presented challenges and problems concerning the quality of schooling: a large number of overage children and youths, high dropout rates, and questionable achievement. Qualified teachers to meet the expanded demands are not available, and although extraordinary efforts are being undertaken to recruit, retain, and upgrade teachers, skilled and socially committed teachers will remain in short supply for some time. The burden of a spate of educational reforms falls on the shoulders of a poorly trained teaching force.

Herculean efforts by MED to revise and improve curricula, publish and disseminate national texts, and endow schools with more adequate learning resources also encounter serious, if not intractable, problems. These obstacles are the consequence of decades of underdevelopment and, since 1981, U.S.-backed military aggression and economic sanctions. As of late 1984, the government has had to cap allocations to social services and education in order to channel increasingly greater public resources into defense.

It may very well be that adversity will drive the engine forces of creation and transformation in society and schooling. It also is very likely that the greatest teacher of political and moral lessons, as in the past, will be the very forces that threaten the Sandinista revolution: the continuing legacies of underdevelopment, the precarious situation of Nicaragua in the world economy, the hegemonic policies of the United States and its continued attempts to shape the internal affairs of the country. The social engagement of many youth, their intense involvement in defense and production activities, may have a greater effect on their social values and political behavior than will all the formal lessons of schools. The social impact of transformations in schooling, even the most promising ones described in this chapter, pale in comparison to the likely effects on youth of the new roles they now play in national life.

The new education system exists in the minds of planners. After five years of reform plans and enthusiastic efforts to give birth to a transformed school system, there is still little substance to those dreams. Elements of what a new system might look like are found in more participatory learning arrangements, in work-study projects, in the rural education *núcleos* that tend to break down the walls between school and community, and in the national science fairs in which talented youth can make a contribution to the society. But all these reforms also are in incipient stages of development. In the meantime, the evolving—and often rapidly changing—national reality requires rapid responses from the education system that may or may not be forthcoming. Moreover, national-level administrators frequently have to make decisions without the opportunity or means to follow up and correct mistakes.

But it is also the case that the Ministry of Education is organizationally a more coherent and effective instrument for responding to the emerging issues of the day. Even the most perceptive and trenchant of critics of the Ministry of Education and its tendency to promote an "ideology of schooling" note that qualitatively there is a much improved and more just education system. As former Vice-Minister of Education Miguel de Castilla Urbina notes, if one judges schooling by its victims, then the post-1979 system of education is beyond question superior, as it has done much to reach out and serve the interests of the most disadvantaged sectors of society.[42]

A transformed education system, in the sense of a new system that substitutes for the previous one,[43] does not exist. Many of the elements of the previous school system—administrative personnel and teachers, as well as traditional expectations of students and parents—are still present. But the goals, symbols, and thrust of educational leadership is definitely in new directions. Whether or not the majority of people, the intended beneficiaries of these reforms, feel that they have a stake in the new system remains a key question.

NOTES

1. Carlos Tünnermann Bernheim, "Cinco Años de Educación en la Revolución," (Managua: Ministiry of Education, 1984).

2. Xabier Gorostiaga, "Dilemma of the Nicaraguan Revolution," in *The Future of Central America,* ed. Richard Fagen and Olga Pellicer (Stanford: Stanford University Press, 1983), pp. 48–51.

3. MED, *Consulta Nacional para Obtener Criterios que Ayuden a Definir los Fines y Objetivos de la Educación Nicaragüense, Informe Preliminar* (Managua: Ministry of Education, August 1981), p. 79.

4. For example, the USSR has made major contributions to the construction and equipping of the Simón Bolívar Energy Institute in Managua, the Agroindustrial Institute in Sebaca, the Mining Institute in Bonanza, the Fishing and Navigation Institute in Bluefields, the La Salle Technical Institute and the Mechanical Agricultural Institute in León; the German Democratic Republic

(East Germany) has been a principal funding source for the Polytechnic Institute of Jinotepe and the Vocational Technical Institute of Managua; Sweden, for the Forestry Institute of San Ramon; and Spain, for the technological institute of Granada. Of the various institutes funded by the USSR, only the Simón Bolívar Energy Institute was in operation in 1984.

5. MED, *Política y Lineamientos,* p. 52.

6. Ibid., p. 56.

7. Margaret E. Crahan, "Varieties of Faith: Religion in Contemporary Nicaragua," Working Paper No. 5, Occidental College, December 1983.

8. Tünnermann, "Cinco Años," p. 23.

9. Interviews in Zwerling and Martin, *Nicaragua,* p. 69.

10. Carlos Tünnermann Bernheim, "La Gestión Educativa en Cinco Años de Revolución," (Managua: Ministry of Education, May 1984), p. 9.

11. Barndt, "Popular Education," p. 330.

12. But frequently the distances to be covered are great and NERs, no matter how well planned, may not be able to reach most of the students in the locale. For example, the NER in the rural area surrounding the town of Rama covers approximately 250 square kilometers and 106 hamlets with 1 base, 1 sub-base, and 12 satellite schools; the NER is able to serve 1,570 students. Still, 40 percent of the students are beyond its coverage.

13. Max H. Minano García, *Proyecto Piloto de Educación Fundamental del Río Coco* (Managua: Ministry of Public Instruction, 1960).

14. MED, "Proyecto de Educación Bilingüe-Bicultural. Plan de Trabajo Junio-Diciembre 1984," (Puerto Cabezas: Zona Especial I, May 21, 1984).

15. David Myers, "Nicaragua," *Mesoamerica* 4 (April 1985), p. 7.

16. Comments of Beatriz D'Ambrozio, a Brazilian doctoral student in the School of Education, Indiana University, Bloomington.

17. Interview with Edgar Jerez Talavero, Ministry of Education, May 1984.

18. The three levels of degrees are the following:

a) OH (*Obrero Habilitado*)—a semi-skilled worker with six years of primary schooling or equivalent and specific skill training.

b) OC (*Obrero Calificado*)—a skilled worker with six years of basic education plus three years of specific skill training.

c) TM (*Técnico Medio*)—a middle-level technician with nine years of basic education plus three years of specific skill training.

19. Interview with Emigdio Reyes, Ministry of Education, June 1984.

20. MED, *Política y Lineamientos,* p. 77.

21. MED, *Política y Lineamientos,* p. 9.

22. These traits are listed in Tünnermann, "Gestión Educativa," p. 10; and in MED, *Educación en Quatro Años de Revolución,* (Managua: Ministry of Education, 1983), pp. 20–23.

23. Samuel Bowles, "Cuban Education and the Revolutionary Ideology," *Harvard Educational Review* 41 (November 1971): 477–78.

24. Ibid; also see Michael Apple, *Education and Power* (London: Routledge & Kegan Paul, 1982), esp. chap. 3; and Pierre Bourdieu and J.C. Passerow, *Reproduction* (Beverly Hills, CA: Sage Publications, 1977); and Henry Giroux, *Ideology, Culture and the Process of Schooling* (Philadelphia: Temple University Press, 1984), pp. 72–78.

25. On the norms of independence and achievement, see Talcott Parsons, "The School Class as a Social System," *Harvard Educational Review* 29 (1959): 297–308; and Robert Dreeben, *On What Is Learned in School* (Reading, Mass.: Addison Wesley, 1968).

26. The student monitors are not supposed to have leadership responsibilities in the Sandinista youth organizations as this would conflict with their academic responsibilities.

27. See, for example, James S. Coleman, *The Adolescent Society* (New York: Free Press, 1961), and Sarane S. Boocock, *An Introduction to the Sociology of Learning* (New York: Houghton, Mifflin, 1982 ed.), pp. 212–41.

28. I am indebted to my research assistant, Frank Barquero of the Ministry of Education, for these insights.

29. MED, "*Orientaciones Generales para Lograr la Participación de los Alumnos en Tareas Socialmente Útiles y el Cuidado de la Propiedad Social*" (Managua: Division of Primary Education, June 20, 1985).

30. MISURASATA leader Steadman Fagoth Mueller, with the largest following, subsequently renamed his faction of counterrevolutionaries, MISURA; the group was based in Honduras. Brooklyn Rivera, who heads the minority faction, MISURASATA, was based in Costa Rica. In the fall of 1984 he began negotiations with the Sandinista government to reach an accord by which the group of Miskito Indians fighting with him may return to Nicaragua under conditions satisfactory to all contending parties. These negotiations broke off in the spring of 1985.

31. For further discussion on the extent of participation, see *Consulta Nacional,* pp. 9–14.

32. Ibid., p. 79.

33. Ibid., p. 134.

34. Ibid., p. 128.

35. Interview with Carlos Tünnermann Bernheim at his home in Managua, June 13, 1984; also see Juan Bautista Arríen, "Plan de Actividades Conjuntas en la Comunidad Educativa del 20 de Agosto al 16 de Septiembre," in his *Nicaragua: Revolución y Projecto Educativo* (Managua: Ministry of Education, 1980), pp. 183–90.

36. The Office of Rural Nuclearization prepares some of the most detailed maps on rural areas available to municipal officials and educators.

37. MED, "Plan Operativo para Estructurar el Modelo de Participación Popular" (Managua: Departamento de Nuclearización Educativa Rural, March 20, 1984).

38. Interview with William Alemán, Ministry of Education, May 31, 1984.

39. Ironically, it is also the school attended by guerrilla commander Jaime Wheelock, Minister of Agriculture and Agrarian Reform, and one of the nine members of the FSLN National Directorate, and by Minister of Education Fernando Cardenal.

40. "Estudiantes Cristianos para la Defensa," *El Nuevo Diario,* June 20, 1984. Interview with Roger Zamora.

41. Ibid.

42. Interview with Miguel de Castilla Urbina, Managua, June 5, 1984.

43. MED, *Política y Lineamientos,* p. 6.

5
Higher Education: Expansion, Improvement, and Transformation

Higher education represents the most critical and the most problematic level of the entire education system. It is critical because it is the most immediately relevant to the human resource needs of the country for highly competent professionals, and because universities in Nicaragua, as elsewhere in Latin America, have been recruiting grounds for political leaders. It is problematic because the post-1979 government inherited a poorly developed and largely undistinguished higher education system, its primary role being to certify existing elites and provide social mobility for a limited number of aspiring and talented youth from nonelite backgrounds. During the Somoza period, the contribution of universities to the so-called "manpower needs" of capitalist development was not very significant. The vast majority of university students were not enrolled in fields directly related to economic growth.

In addition to the underdeveloped state of higher education inherited from the Somoza period, the current system encounters a number of problems resulting from the deficiencies of lower levels of schooling. These deficiencies are readily acknowledged by higher education planning officials to include the following: "the weak preparation in Basic Sciences and Mathematics, low quality of faculty, limited or nearly nonexistent vocational formation and occupational orientation on the part of the Ministry of Education, inadequate resource base, lack of study habits and little inclination toward experimental work, slow transformation of academic plans and programs. . . ."[1]

While facing serious constraints, the Nicaraguan higher education system also has undergone a significant expansion, made noticeable improvements in a number of areas, and has been transformed to accord with radical changes in the political economy of the country. As in previous chapters, accomplishments over the past five years will be analyzed in

107

relation to challenges, constraints, and contradictions—with attention given to those problems created by the reform process itself.

EXPANSION

In 1978, there were 23,791 students enrolled in four universities and six higher education institutions forming part of the Nicaraguan Association of Higher Education. The four universities were the National Autonomous University (*Universidad Nacional Autónoma de Nicaragua,* UNAN), with campuses in León and Managua; the Central American University (*Universidad Centroamericana,* UCA); the Polytechnic University (*Universidad Politécnica,* UPOLI); and the Private University of Higher Studies (*Universidad Privada Autonoma de Estudios Superiores,* UPACES). The other higher education institutions were the School of Commercial Studies (*Centro de Ciencias Comerciales,* CCC); the School of Public Accountants of Managua (*Escuela de Contadores Públicos de Nicaragua,* ECPN); the National School of Nursing (*Escuela Nacional de Enfermería,* ENE); the National Center of Education and Sciences (*Centro Nacional de Educación y Ciencias,* CENEC); the Nicaraguan Technological Institute of Higher Studies (*Instituto Tecnológico de Estudios Superiores de Nicaragua,* ITESNIC); and the Central American Institute of Business Administration (*Instituto Centroamericano de Administración de Empresas,* INCAE), that served as a regional school.

By 1983, the higher education system had expanded to 39,765 students; and by 1984, to an estimated 41,237[2] in four universities, one extension campus (in education in Estelí), and 12 technical training centers. There were two national research centers and six hospitals serving as training institutions for doctors, dentists, and nurses. Altogether, the government had created nine new higher education centers. The two campuses of UNAN (in León and Managua) each became a separate autonomous, degree-granting university. UCA continued as a private institution with substantial public subsidization. A new National Engineering University (*Universidad Nacional de Ingeniería,* UNI) was opened in 1983. Among the institutions closed by the new government were CCC, ECPN, ENE, CENEC, UPACES. Reasons for terminating these centers include poor quality, duplication of scarce resources, and irrelevance to national development plans.

Along with the expansion of student enrollments and facilities, there has been a substantial increase in faculty. In the academic year 1980–81 there were 1,474 faculty (an increase of approximately 400 over the prerevolutionary period); in 1984, there were 1,750 faculty and over 700 students working as teaching assistants.

The most dramatic increase has been in government financing of higher education. In 1979, the last year of the Somoza government, 58.3 million cordobas had been authorized for the following year's higher education expenses. By 1984, allocations were seven times higher and included both public and private institutions; state financing of higher education accounted for 94 percent of all expenditures. In 1978, state support per student was 1,524 cordobas; by 1984, it had risen to 12,259 cordobas, an eightfold increase over the pre-revolutionary period.

With less than 4 percent of total school enrollments, higher education received almost one-fifth of all state allocations. In this sense, students who attend higher education institutions are indeed privileged. The state spends more than eight times as much on a higher education student than on a high school student, and ten times more than on a primary school student.

Higher education students universally represent a privileged minority, both with regard to benefits and opportunities. But it is also the case in post-1979 Nicaragua that decisive steps have been taken to broaden the social class composition of the student body. Access has been considerably democratized by charging no tuition other than a nominal matriculation fee of 136 córdobas to cover the costs of a student identification card and a contribution to student government; by instituting a quota system to guarantee enrollments from all regions of the country, especially the most underrepresented; and by establishing a Preparatory Faculty (*Facultad Preparatoria,* FP) to provide an accelerated high school program to students who otherwise would not be able to attend a university.

Despite these democratizing efforts (which will be described in greater detail in subsequent sections of this chapter), a plurality of students today are still from middle-class and elite backgrounds. Precise data are not available on the social class origins of entering students. But given the past advantages of middle- and upper-class students with regard to the quality of their primary and secondary schooling, and the greater likelihood of their passing entrance examinations, in addition to their ability to forego work in order to study full time, it will be some time before working-class students constitute a majority.

A principal factor impeding the spread of opportunity is the limited number of fellowships available due to the worsening economic situation in the country. The number of fellowships for the national universities in Managua and León has been capped at 2,400 with 600 fellowships available for the agricultural programs in Rivas and Estelí. Other state entities provide an additional 800 fellowships. Taking into account 1,800 fellowships for study abroad (the great majority in socialist countries), the total number of fellowships available in 1984 was 5,600.[3] Altogether, less than one-sixth of all higher education students studying either within the country or overseas received direct state assistance.

With the expansion and the enormous influx of students immediately following the reopening of universities in 1979–80, there have been problems. Not unlike lower levels of schooling, promotion rates have been very low. In 1980–81, approximately one-half (49.7 percent) of students did not have to repeat courses and continued on to the next course level. Over one-fourth (28.6 percent) dropped out. By 1983, the promotion rate had increased to 57 percent. The national government in the intervening years had initiated a study of academic performance. Seventeen national commissions consisting of representatives of MED, ANDEN, the National Union of Nicaraguan Students (*Union Nacional de Estudiantes Nicaragüenses,* UNEN), and MIPLAN studied various aspects of retention rates.

Among the reasons given for the low promotion rates were inadequate academic resources, poorly prepared faculty, excessive academic demands placed on students combined with constant mobilizations of youth for defense and production tasks, a disjointed curriculum and chaotic credit system, and inadequate evaluation procedures for both students and faculty. The response to these problems is described in the subsequent sections on improvements and transformations in higher education.

IMPROVEMENTS

Principal among the improvements are increased capital allocations to instructional resources and facilities, the reorganization and revision of curricula in conjunction with efforts to upgrade faculty, and the establishment of a higher education planning body, CNES (*Consejo Nacional de la Educación Superior*) to coordinate higher education policy with national development priorities.

Capital Improvements

Higher education, which had been poorly endowed during the Somoza period (in part because of student opposition to the dictatorship), was in an absolutely devastated condition in mid-1979.[4] The National University (at León and Managua) had been a virtual battleground during the period 1978–79. Even the better endowed Central American University, which subsequent to the 1972 Managua earthquake had part of its physical plant built with Inter-American Development Bank funds, still has a number of classrooms in temporary quonset hut-type facilities. Generally speaking, library and laboratory facilities in UNAN and UCA were in extremely poor condition.

Of the vastly increased expenditures for higher education, 20 percent is presently allocated to capital development. Much of the capital investment has gone into classroom construction, with expenditures for this purpose 12.4 times greater in 1983 than in 1979. An increase from 2.18 square meters per student in 1979 to 3.64 in 1983 is one indicator of physical plant expansion, which, according to CNES, is still not an optimum amount of space per student.

As with classroom space, the number of books per student is still very limited, with fewer than five books per higher education student in 1984. This figure means that in many classes students do not have their own texts. The number of books in libraries is inadequate and, as is often the case in Latin America, many are in English.

Many instructors have had to distribute mimeographed copies of their lecture notes, develop their own classroom manuals or cut up existing texts and duplicate them. In many instances, these various "pirated" materials serve as a stop-gap measure; in some cases, however, improvisation has led to improved materials that are more oriented to current problems and involve more active student learning since they are geared to field work.

Emphasis on curriculum development has led to the production of basic texts in biology, Spanish, mathematics, and the History of the Popular Sandinista Revolution. Undeniably, there has been a spate of home-produced Nicaraguan texts in the areas of national history and political economy that accord with Sandinista perspectives and priorities for development.

Moreover, as part of national higher education plans that specify expected enrollments by field and numbers of fellowships within and outside the country, there is a category for the number of books to be published locally and on the international market. The 1984 plan, for example, details the need to purchase 2,300 texts in agricultural sciences (2,000 to be acquired abroad), and similarly 2,500 in medical sciences (of which only 100 will be published locally).

These conditions—greatly expanded enrollments, a nontraditional student body, and the lack of ready-made classroom learning materials—places tremendous demands on the teaching force. Unfortunately, as with lower levels of education, many of the higher education faculty are very young and inexperienced.

Upgrading Faculty

Several factors have contributed to the rather skewed composition of Nicaragua's higher education faculty. A significant problem for the system is directly attributable to the needs of the revolutionary government for competent and committed individuals. Over 200 faculty, including some of the most experienced and talented academics in the country, left their university appointments to work in key decision posts.[5] These and other departures, coupled with the dramatic increase in number of academic positions, have created a situation in which over three-fourths of higher education faculty now working have been employed only since 1979. Their average age in 1984, when over 80 percent of them were under 30, was 28 years. But their youth and inexperience are not the only problems: in 1984, there were fewer than five Nicaraguans with doctorates teaching in higher education programs. In many scientific areas there were no faculty with advanced graduate training. According to CNES, a substantial number of faculty lack "scientific, technical, pedagogical, and political and ideological preparation."[6]

Higher education authorities faced with this situation have allocated a substantial portion of operating expenditures to recruit, retrain, and upgrade faculty, as well as restructure working conditions and raise expectations for faculty performance. Salaries have been increased, teaching loads have been prescribed, and inservice training programs have been developed.

To attract more talented people into the profession, steps have been taken to establish the foundations of a salary schedule. On the basis of academic credentials alone, faculty advance through seven levels of remuneration that start at a base of 6,500 cordobas monthly and ascend to 9,000 cordobas per month for full-time appointments. High-level administrators and highly qualified foreign faculty may earn up to 10,000 cordobas monthly.

Increasing the number of full-time faculty devoting their energies and talents to teaching, research, and community service has been another priority of higher education authorities. Prior to 1979, over 80 percent of faculty were employed on an hourly or part-time basis. In 1980–81, 44 percent of the total of 1,474 faculty were full time. By 1983, the situation had begun to turn around: 60 percent were full time. In 1984, CNES plans called for 70 percent of the more than 1,750 faculty to be working on a full-time basis.

Establishing guidelines for teaching loads is another effort aimed at improving the quality of faculty and making careers in higher education more attractive. The teaching load for full-time faculty has been set at a maximum of two separate courses per semester with approximately 15 contact hours per week. In addition, faculty are to be available ten hours a week for student consultation.[7]

Ongoing inservice activities also are a systematic part of national, university, and departmental plans. In the universities, faculty are expected to invest four to eight hours a week in the improvement of their teaching and research activities. In 1984, CNES estimates that 80 percent of higher educational personnel had been involved in various forms of inservice training since efforts had been instituted in 1980. For 1984 alone, CNES plans called for approximately 70 percent of faculty to be involved in inservice courses that it was organizing.

Beyond the professional deficiencies, the present government assigns significant weight to political commitment. A memorial statement for a fourth-year engineering professor who had been mobilized for duty in the war zone illustrates the emphasis placed on the engaged academic.

> Education workers are, by essence, carriers of an ideology, that is to say, reproducers of conceptions, ideas, values which are identified with a determined class. In our case, we ought to be bearers of the ideas of Sandino, reproducers of Sandino, predicators of the historic programs of the worker and of the FSLN.
> As educators we ought to make out actions correspond to our ideas.[8]

At the same time, it would be a mistake to believe that political fervor without technical competence is condoned by authorities within the university community. Moreover, faculty are not lightly excused from their teaching responsibilities to engage in political activities. Although regulations are not always followed, a teacher who wishes to miss even one hour of class to participate in, for example, a mobilization must have the permission of university officials.[9] Similarly, students involved in various mobilizations are not to be accorded special favors by faculty or have academic standards applied to them any less rigorously.

Faculty members outwardly hostile to the current regime are unlikely to be employed. But professionally competent and politically apathetic instructors are tolerated. Generally, however, considerable effort is invested in political consciousness raising as part of inservice activities to upgrade faculty.

The above picture of university life in post-1979 Nicaragua suggests that for pedagogical as well as political reasons faculty are regulated and controlled to an extent that would be considered intolerable in most U.S. higher education institutions. Higher education authorities, as well as many students, however, claim that these controls are necessary to guarantee that teachers cover basic material, to ensure a certain standard of instruction, and to promote an orderly academic environment free of constant changes in course offerings and graduation requirements. These controls are built into the new academic organization of higher education and curriculum plans.

Academic Reorganization and Curricular Changes

Among the significant changes in higher education are the elimination of general studies and the introductory year of general studies, and the formulation of study plans for each field of specialization. The plans set forth in detail the sequence of courses students are to take, the objectives and content of each course, the amount of time to be allocated to lecture, recitation, laboratory, and practical experiences. These study plans correspond to occupational profiles prepared by national commissions of leading experts in a field of study. The profiles specify the types of knowledge and skills necessary for competence in a particular career. Faculty are expected to closely follow the plans with regard to content, activities, and allocation of time for defined topics.

Besides the close linkage to economic decision making, a number of the reasons for these study plans have already been discussed. They include a young and poorly prepared teaching force which, it is claimed, will benefit from a well designed curriculum planned by specialists. Given past abuses by faculty, the still considerable number of part-time faculty, and the constant disruptions in academic life generated by the revolutionary environment, certain minimal curriculum requirements must be mandated. Also, the study plans indicate areas where outside expertise must be sought and national competence developed if the higher education system is to prepare qualified professionals.

Students also do not have the freedom to design their own programs. The credit system, according to CNES officials, allowed students to proceed through a curriculum at their own pace with many falling behind or taking extended periods to complete their studies. Under the present system, once students come on track, their schedule of courses is laid out for the duration of their studies. Moreover, if students fail two courses they must repeat the year. This may be done two times before being required to leave the university.

Reasons for the elimination of the general studies requirement are not as easily ascertainable. Since the academic preparation of incoming students appears to be no better than before, it would seem that the need for an introductory orientation is still valid. But the new government first reduced the year of general studies and by the 1982 academic year had eliminated it entirely. One reason may be the need for students to commence their professional studies immediately. Another might be that the previous system of general studies, along with the semester plan credit hours, and electives—all of which introduce choice and flexibility for students—is associated with past U.S. influences on the higher education system. These influences, promoted by USAID and large philanthropic foundations like Ford,[10] attempted to transplant elements of the U.S. university model to Latin America, which had been heavily influenced by the

Napoleonic model of higher education institutions geared to the state's human resource needs. In addition to the continuing presence of the Napoleonic model, the current Nicaraguan system is influenced by the Cuban, and indirectly by the Soviet, model of higher education.

Nonetheless, remnants of the previous U.S.-influenced model persist. According to the rector of UCA, some fields of study continue to have a first year of general studies consisting of basic introductory courses but with an orientation geared more toward the specialization.[11]

In line with academic reorganization, standards and demands also have risen. The current semester system of 16 weeks (compared with 14 previously) has increased the number of classroom contact hours per week for daytime students from 21–25 to 26–32. The situation is different for night-time students who previously studied 16–20 hours per week and now face a limit of 16 hours. However, night students must study six years to complete their studies compared with five years for daytime students.

The overall demands per student for classroom hourly attendance and time set aside for final examinations and practical experiences has increased the student load by one-fourth to one-third. With these increased demands, there also has been a decrease in the number of night-time students from 75 percent of enrollments the first year after the revolution to approximately 50 percent in 1984.

Despite efforts to guarantee the quality of instruction and to ensure through a highly-structured curriculum that basic areas of knowledge are covered, the initial results are mixed. According to CNES, in addition to the shortage of educational materials caused by lack of foreign exchange, problems have arisen because a great number of courses are not offered and classes are often suspended in disorganized and arbitrary fashion,[12] due to the various upheavals and mobilizations that characterize the revolutionary situation in the country. Also, despite the best efforts of the study plan authors, students are overloaded with unnecessary information. CNES attributes the failure to implement study plans to faculty "indiscipline" and "excessive liberalism."[13]

In 1984, however, implementation of the study plans in all specializations was going to be obligatory, with (supposedly) severe sanctions for professors who arbitrarily deviated from them. Whether greater bureaucratic control over faculty, straight-jacketing them with minimally-defined study plans, will resolve qualitative problems of higher education in Nicaragua is problematic. Even students who recognize some of the positive outcomes of the study plans express concerns over teaching that is reduced to simplistic and mechanistic delivery of prescribed materials. At the highest level of the Ministry of Education and other governmental entities involved with education, there is outspoken criticism of the plans as being antithetical to the nature and mission of a university. It is universally agreed among higher education planners that there is a great need for universities to contribute to the creation of knowledge, and to the expansion of intellectual horizons as well as to the raising of critical consciousness. But it is questionable that the technocratic and bureaucratic policies that have been set in motion to standardize instruction in accordance with a factory model of education will accomplish these lofty goals.

Fortunately, these bureaucratizing forces do not have a stranglehold on creativity. There are many encouraging signs of teacher inventiveness in redesigning and adapting curricula to fit changing times, in encouraging students to be more inquiry oriented and to have confidence that they can contribute to scientific invention and practice as well as to cultural creation and expression. Faculty themselves, for the very first time, may also be engaged in research and involved in the application of knowledge to the resolution of social problems. Various departments and higher education institutions are on the cutting edge of knowledge generation and application in Nicaragua in such fields as fisheries and aquaculture, forest ecology, nutritional sciences, and biochemistry.[14]

Realistically, however, it should also be recognized that there are serious resource constraints. Even with expanded investments in higher education, capital expenditures constitute only 20 percent of a limited budget. Working conditions do not afford what is considered bare essentials in certain specializations. The conditions in Nicaragua are not unlike those in other underdeveloped countries: electricity frequently shuts down, telephone lines may not be working for months, heavy rains may cause mud slides blocking entrances to campuses, photocopying machines—even typewriters—are luxuries. Essential books, scholarly journals, and laboratory equipment are not available because of lack of foreign exchange.

One result is that student academic performance is still not of a very high caliber overall. The dropout rate has been reduced but still hovers at about 15 percent. Those who do graduate—and by 1984, the higher education system had graduated some 7,900 professionals and technicians—may still not represent the new Nicaraguan person dedicated to the collective well being rather than self-advancement, although they may represent an amalgam of old and new. These transformations in the characteristics of graduates depend on transformations in the character of higher education, which may not yet have been realized.

TRANSFORMATIONS

Over the past five years, there have been significant efforts to transform the social relations of learning. Even more significant, in the case of higher education, is the dramatic restructuring of higher education to accord with economic and social priorities of the revolutionary government.

Higher education has a whole new cast and hue. Higher education during the Somoza period may have been loosely coupled with the incipient stages of industrialization and an emergent dependent capitalism,[15] and this is especially evident in the creation of the Central American University in 1960–61. In contrast, the present system has been dramatically reoriented to dovetail with the goals of the Sandinista government to achieve a more egalitarian and prosperous country, and more autonomous national development serving, first and foremost, the vast majority of Nicaraguans. In the revamping process, higher education has acquired many of the characteristics of the Soviet model, which is based on a planned economy and specialization of higher education institutions. Notable features of this model include the alignment of enrollment patterns, curricular organization and content with human resource plans. With the exception of Cuba, this technocratic, "manpower planning" approach to higher education is rare in Latin America. The instrument for bringing higher education into alignment with national development plans is CNES, which in and of itself must be considered a major transformation in the higher education system.

CNES and Higher Education Planning

CNES, the National Higher Education Council, was created by Decree #325 of March 4, 1980, as the "policy-making and planning body for higher education . . . [to] respond to the demand for a skilled work force required by the process of National Reconstruction and the construction of a New Nicaraguan Society."[16]

CNES consists of representatives of all major higher education institutions, as well as executive officers of the National Union of Nicaraguan Students (UNEN), the National Association of Nicaraguan Educators (ANDEN), and the Sandinista Workers' Confederation (CST). Overseeing the policies of CNES is the National Education Council. The overall thrust of CNES, therefore, accords with the educational policies and directives of the highest levels of the party and the state.

Unlike many higher education governing and policy bodies in Latin America, CNES would appear to have extraordinary powers in its ability to close down or open up institutions, departments, and programs. The unprecedented authority of CNES is also manifest in the role it has played in developing the five-year study plans for all major career areas. The streamlining of higher education institutions and programs, enrollment patterns in different fields of study, and the growth of technical education are all testaments to the power of the council. CNES also has played a principal role in formulating policies and regulations governing admissions, financial aid, student and faculty conduct, and faculty evaluation and promotion.

Although CNES is not a ministry, its president has accumulated and exercised so much authority that he is sometimes treated as a de facto minister. The extent of this authority, as well as the substance and technocratic thrust of CNES policies, may go against the traditional grain and may antagonize many educators of a different persuasion concerning the goals and nature of higher education. But CNES, nonetheless, has left its mark on the system.

Higher Education and Human Resource Plans

According to the present leadership of the country, higher education during the Somoza years was poorly planned and tenuously related to national development. There was duplication of efforts with a proliferation of programs in fields like business administration, which were frequently run as profit-making enterprises, and a surfeit of students in economics, social sciences, humanities, and law. In 1978–79, these fields claimed 60 percent of enrollments. At the same time, there were insufficient enrollments and institutional offerings in key areas such as agricultural sciences, technology, and education.

Among the first steps taken by the new government was the closing down of five institutions of higher education. Programs such as administration and accounting, which were offered in three or more institutions, were consolidated and placed in one institution in order to eliminate duplication of scarce resources. Other examples of consolidation of effort include moving the medical faculty of UNAN from León to Managua in 1982, and the journalism faculty from the Rubén Darío campus of UNAN/Managua to the Ricardo Morales Aviles campus of UCA in 1984. Moreover, some 21 university fields of study (out of a total of 130 undergraduate offerings) are in the process of being closed down. However, some fields that were initially closed down, such as social work, are now being reopened.

Among the most impressive shifts in higher education over the past five years are the rapidly expanding enrollments in the four priority areas designated by the national government. The fields of agricultural sciences, medical sciences, education sciences, and technology which comprised less than half (42 percent) of the enrollments in 1980, represented 70 percent of enrollments as of 1984. Each one of these fields attracted between 15 and 18 percent of higher education enrollments. By contrast, enrollments in the humanities, social sciences, economics, and law had declined to approximately 27 percent.

One incentive for students to enroll in priority areas is the greater availability of fellowships. The 2,400 fellowships allotted to UNAN are exclusively for these areas, and another 600 are set aside for agricultural studies in Estelí and Rivas.

Policies not only encourage enrollment in development related fields, but are designed to attract students to such specializations from all regions of the country. For example, of the 550 first-year positions open in medicine in 1984, 370 were reserved for students from the Pacific Coast Region, 150 from the North Central Zone, and 30 from the Atlantic Coast Region.

Another significant shift is is in the direction of more students studying at nonuniversity institutions of higher education. Students enrolled in various technical institutes accounted for approximately one-fifth (18 percent) of all postsecondary enrollments in 1984, but nearly one-third of new entrants. In 1979, there were only three higher technical education centers; in 1984 there were 12.

Technical education will continue to grow and enroll a larger share of higher education students. Besides the subprofessional and technical specializations that offer a TS (*Técnico Superior*) degree in two and a half or three years, there is a National Engineering University (UNI), which offers seven engineering careers, and there is a Superior Institute of Agricultural Sciences (*Instituto Superior de Ciencias Agropecuarias,* ISCA). In 1983, UNI began offering the first two years of engineering courses, as UNAN and UCA started to phase out their engineering programs.[17] Plans for transferring programs to ISCA, on the Northern Highway outside Managua, were on the drawing board in 1984. Other projections called for the training of technical school teachers to be located in UPOLI.

Long-range plans under consideration for the restructuring of higher education call for greater specialization and a reduced role for universities in human resource formation in technological areas. UNAN, for example, would be streamlined to become a center for superior studies in natural and physical sciences and the social sciences, as well as the center for a national science academy. Medicine would be transferred to a Higher Institute of Medical Sciences; education would be transferred to a Higher Institute of Pedagogical Sciences. UCA would specialize in humanities, law, and public and business administration.

While specialization is called for at the undergraduate level, there is considerable debate between MED, CNES, MIPLAN, and various ministries over postgraduate specialization and where it should be offered. In 1983, there were only some 406 students in 18 postgraduate programs, 80 percent of them in medical sciences. For now, the group advocating overseas study for advanced specialization in such fields as textile technology has prevailed. Given the availability of fellowships for study in Eastern European countries and the USSR, this means that approximately 90 percent of advanced work abroad will be in these countries. Poor relations between the United States and Nicaragua and specific punitive actions of the United States, such as the cessation of USAID funding for programs like LASPAU (Latin American Scholarship Program of American Universities), are only part of the reason. Extreme foreign exchange limitations are also significant. Despite the recognition on the part of a number of high-level decision makers in Nicaragua that it would be desirable for their professionals to be exposed to different models of higher education and to be able to study in certain fields in which U.S. institutions may be superior, there will be few opportunities for Nicaraguans to engage in advanced study in the United States.

What now prevails is the Cuban-cum Soviet-style model of higher education with its emphasis on close correspondence between superior studies and human resource plans. The limitations of the "manpower forecasting" model have been documented elsewhere[18] and are difficult to implement even in a "command economy," which Nicaragua definitely is not.[19] But even if this engineering approach to higher education (controlling the number of students in particular fields at a given time) were to be free of many of its inherent problems (e.g., the lag between the need for so many people in such and such fields in year x and the time actually required to train such people), the data base for such planning is extremely deficient in Nicaragua. Precise five- or ten-year economic plans are not available as guidelines for the education system, nor has MED been able to project data on the number of students who will be completing different levels of education in a given time so that supply and demand can be meshed.[20] Other problems include the need for higher education decision makers to continually respond to crises rather than to concentrate on long-range planning.[21] Moreover, hasty decision making may have led to some mistakes, such as terminating social work (which then had to be reopened as a specialization) and the field of pedagogy in the UNAN/School of Education when there is a tremendous need for expertise in this area.

Beyond specific difficulties and shortcomings is the question of the desirability of the technocratic, "scientific" approach to higher education, and in treating advanced studies in primarily economic terms. Furthermore, there is a tendency on the part of some human resource and education planners to view all fields of studies as sciences. It is questionable if the humanities, and even such fields as the social "sciences," can be forced into the mold of the physical and natural sciences; assuming that this were possible, the appropriateness of doing so is doubtful. It is this technocratic bent, however, which shapes not only admissions policies and study plans but also the social relations of learning.

Social Relations of Learning

Many of the reforms attempted at lower levels of the school system (study groups, collective assignments, more active learning) also are being tested in higher education. The results are no more encouraging, nor depressing, in higher education institutions than they are in primary and secondary schools. The same restraints obtain: the lack of books and laboratory facilities for more student-centered, inquiry-oriented learning, the absence of an appropriate methodology for group-based study, and the prevalence of inexperienced teachers.

What has changed is the degree of verticality or hierarchy in teacher-student interactions. There has been a significant curtailment of the authority and autonomy of teachers. This shift is all the more striking in the light of the once magisterial, if not imperious, status and stance of past university professors. Not only is there less distance between teachers and students, but in some respects the relation has been reversed, with students now exercising a certain amount of control over teachers.

The CNES-developed study plans specifying what is to be taught, when, and how[22] are, in part, responsible for this reversal. Regulations require that on the first day of classes the instructor acquaint each class with the course study plan of the semester. Theoretically, students have the right to complain to departmental heads and institutional officials when the faculty member deviates from the plan, although this can be negotiated with the students.

That these study plans are not to be flouted is all the more evident in steps taken by departmental and institutional authorities to regulate daily instruction. According to Article 34 of the Higher Education Academic Code, instructors are required to submit a lesson plan to either department heads or the principal professors of a course, specifying the objectives and content of instruction. The standardized lesson plan form, to be filled out by the instructor, is detailed to the point of disclosing what will be discussed during the introductory, middle, and concluding sections of the class.

In certain departments there has been widespread resistance to filling out these forms. Moreover, high-status faculty, particularly specialists in the medical school, are not requested to comply, as it is assumed by administrators that they are competent professionals.

Another element of contention in student-faculty relations is that many students feel confident to challenge their instructors with regard to technical competence as well as political commitment. Earlier chapters mentioned the initial tension that existed between the youth ("*los muchachos*") who were veteran combatants and their teachers who had not engaged in armed struggle to overthrow the Somoza regime. Such tension also exists at the higher education level. It is compounded by the fact that many higher education students work during the day and study at night, that they often have accumulated valuable work experience, and that they are more or less the same age as their instructors. Older faculty, who stayed on after the change of regimes and who may not share the same political ideas and enthusiasm as the more militant members of the Sandinista youth organizations, also come under challenge.

It would be a mistake, however, to concentrate on the element of lost faculty authority or even antagonistic student-faculty relations. The primary shift may be in the direction of closer faculty-student relations in which faculty truly serve as mentors of fledgling members of a profession. Such a situation is possible because a greater percentage of faculty teach full time, an important component of academic work loads consists of supervising work-study and practical experiences, and greater emphasis is placed on the application of scientific theory and course knowledge to concrete social situations. Moreover, many faculty and students share the same political commitments and are jointly involved in defense and production activities. They may also work together as militants of the FSLN.

Contributing to closer student-faculty relations is the Movement of Student Assistants (*Alumnos Ayudantes,* AAs). Given the shortage of instructors that existed in 1979–80, Nicaraguan higher education policy makers, borrowing from the Cuban case, turned to their own students. The decision was made to select and train the most academically competent and socially committed as teaching assistants. Students are chosen at the end of the first year of studies. They serve as teacher aides the next two years and as instructors with significant classroom and laboratory responsibilities the last two years of their academic career. Frequently, these AAs are then sent abroad for graduate study and return as faculty members. The prospect of advanced study overseas is one incentive for assuming the considerable responsibilities of being an AA; other incentives may be the prestige that accompanies such a position, as well as the financial aid that pays room and board and a monthly stipend.

In 1980–81, there were 569 AAs, and in 1983 there were some 780. One effect of this increase has been to lower the student-faculty ratio from 38 to 28 during the period 1980–83. Although the AA movement may be a stop-gap measure, it has a number of positive spin-offs. Unquestionably, many talented students are attracted into higher-education teaching as a career, and they are likely to be more committed and to learn more as a result of the professional responsibilities with which they are entrusted. Many do an excellent job as teachers, establishing more effective personal and pedagogical relations with their students than do regular faculty.

Increases in collegiality and camaraderie are two elements of post-1979 higher education life for both faculty and students. Faculty departments are organized as collectives. Within this structure, faculty may exercise, at least theoretically, some measure of control over their professional lives. For example, if faculty have problems with the existing national study plans and wish to change them, it is possible to modify and adapt them at the level of the departmental collective. It may also be that the collective is a mechanism for controlling faculty at the departmental level.

Because the concept is so new, the direction in which these collectives will go—whether towards greater self-determination or top-down control—is difficult to predict.

Overall, whatever benefits may result from standardizing instruction, the outcomes for faculty development and the nature of higher-education instruction are of questionable value if open, critical, and divergent thinking is a desired outcome.

Relations between higher education, work, and community work-study

At the level of curricular transformation are efforts to overcome the distance between theory and practice, intellectual and manual work. To this end, five weeks per semester are devoted to field work and practical experience. During the first two years of higher education studies, students engage in orientation and "familiarization" visits to work sites (*practicas de familiarización*); during the third and fourth years, they specialize in a particular field of work as apprentices or aides, which culminates in the final and fifth year of study in writing a thesis. Examples of socially valuable and professionally relevant training include social science students conducting housing surveys and recording nutritional deficiencies in school children,[23] law students helping establish and run legal aid clinics for low-income people, and engineering students working in sugar mills.

The most systematic inclusion of community related services as part of professional formation is found in the medical school. Social medicine is offered every semester of the five-year academic program, with students engaging in research projects for periods of up to two months during their fourth and fifth years. Practical experiences are scheduled one-half day per week throughout the entire course of their studies. During their first year of course work, students spend the half day learning to vaccinate and keep records as part of the national health campaigns; the second year, they work in schools; the third year, in community medicine with Sandinista Defense Committees; the fourth year, in occupational medicine, concentrating on problems such as tuberculosis in the workplace; the fifth year, in child and maternal health care centers.[24] Although there are a limited number of professionals to supervise the students, and the student-faculty ratio is much higher than in a U.S. medical school, the Nicaraguan students are entrusted with considerably more responsibility than their North American counterparts. The Nicaraguan students' mark-ups become part of the patients' medical records, which is not the case in the United States.

Not all practical experiences are as relevant and professionally worthwhile as those in medicine. Agreements remain to be worked out between relevant ministries and a number of academic programs to provide meaningful work opportunities. In priority areas like agronomy or agricultural engineering, where there should be an abundance of opportunities for hands-on experience, work-study activities frequently are of little practical value. One student leader quipped that many students in his field would not know what to do with a dismantled tractor, assuming that they were able to recognize one as such.

The work-study component, moreover, places great demands on faculty who supervise student field work and research activities. Most faculty are already overburdened with teaching and administrative, as well as political, activities. Many are poorly prepared to oversee applied scientific work and inquiry activities.

Efforts are under way to upgrade faculty in research methodology, to form a network of "research multipliers" who would assist faculty in this area, and to establish research and development councils in all higher education centers. But these plans are in the initial stages of implementation.

Despite these limitations, the work-study requirements have had a transforming effect on higher education. Curricula unquestionably have been updated. Many faculty and students not only have changed their perceptions of science, but they have acquired the skills and habits to contribute to the systematic accumulation of knowledge.

Science fairs

Complementing the formal curriculum are the co-programmatic or extracurricular activities. In 1982, following the initiation of National Science Fairs at the high school level, similar national competitions were established in the universities. Designated as *Jornadas Universitarias de Desarrollo Científico,* the 1983 science competition involved over 600 students in 121 projects, supervised by 116 faculty. UNEN, a principal sponsor of the fairs, has set a goal of 10 percent of university students participating in the *jornadas.* As with the high school fairs, the general quality of the projects is often undistinguished, but there are a number of exemplary entries that suggest ways in which students can contribute their talents and knowledge and so raise productivity, improve social services, and resolve a variety of everyday problems such as improving sanitary conditions in the dairy industry, or using solar energy to drive machines or dehydrate foods. The *jornadas* are heralded by national authorities and mass organizations such as UNEN and ANDEN as constituting a response to imperialist aggression and as an indication of the important role youth play in national reconstruction.

Mobilizations

The mobilization of youth for defense and production activities is integrally linked to the formal curriculum. Special make-up sessions and examinations have been provided to accommodate these students. Significantly, the national university calendar was changed in 1982 to coincide with the harvest period of major export crops such as coffee. Two months (mid-January to mid-March) have been added to the traditional Christmas-time break to extend the period available for participation in production activities.

Student participation is an expression of patriotic sacrifice and altruistic idealism. But it also is used to satisfy the five-week practical experience in a particular field of study.

Again, the field of medicine offers a valuable case study. In 1982–83, 250 medical students served in combat zones for extended periods of six months or more.[25] After students voiced concern that extended mobilizations would cause them to lose the academic year, university authorities reached an agreement with the army (*Ejército Popular Sandinista,* EPS) and MINSA. The agreement limits mobilization of medical students to 40 days of military-related service at any one time. Student leaders, who had formed a health brigade to serve in combat zones, cite the value of such experience as "putting knowledge . . . into practice and adding a humanistic sense to their profession." According to one student, the son of a tailor, "in a capitalist system this career is . . . for the privileged and those who think of it as a means of profit."[26]

All medical students spend their last two years of study on reserve military status. Upon graduation, they will be required to work for the state in the most impoverished and isolated areas of the country. Traditionally, medical students have had an obligatory period of social service. In 1983, the obligation was extended to graduates of agricultural sciences and education, but for a period of only one year. Efforts of the national government to provide basic services to the distant corners of the country are further bolstered by admissions policies which are designed to recruit students who, for reasons of social class and residence, would not normally have the means to attend a higher education institution.

Facultad Preparatoria

The Preparatory Faculty (FP) represents another major innovation designed to extend opportunity to disadvantaged sectors of the society as well as to those most likely to be politically active and committed to employ their higher studies for social ends. The FP, based on a similar program in

Cuba, provides the equivalent of a high school degree in three years of study for youths, ages 15–25, who are workers, peasants, excombatants of the FSLN, and their children. Mass organizations are solicited to recommend candidates for the FP. In 1984, there were approximately 1,650 students attending classes at the UNAN/Managua–Rubén Darío campus and UNAN/León, with approximately 100 more students in the León program. Virtually all FP students receive lodging and food, and over 90 percent also receive a monthly stipend plus additional expenses for home travel during vacation periods.

The FP represents an interesting attempt to balance political and human resource objectives. Undeniably, the FP serves the purposes of changing the social class composition of the university, and of recruiting politically conscious students who are expected to occupy important positions in the society.[27] These students contribute to the "combativeness" of the student body—a highly prized trait in the eyes of Sandinista leaders. For example, whereas 35–40 percent of day-time students at the UNAN/ Managua might be involved in some form of defense activity (militia or reserve duty), it is estimated that virtually 100 percent of FP students are involved in such actions; and among the 1984 student body there were two subcommanders and a number of captains who studied in the morning and worked in the army in the afternoon and evening.

Another important goal is for these youths to complete the equivalent of secondary education in a condensed period so that they will be able to move into higher studies in priority areas. The objective is that they will contribute knowledge and skills to the development of their communities and regions, which are in dire need of high-level professionals. To facilitate the achievement of these goals, priority faculties reserve a set number of places for FP graduates: medicine, for example, annually sets aside some 40 to 45 places.

Another step that has been taken to ensure the academic success of FP students involves offering a basic curriculum that concentrates on instruction in language, science, mathematics, and technology. Students also learn teaching skills. The teachers in the FP, themselves, are carefully screened to represent some of the most talented and dedicated faculty at the two national universities.

University authorities claim that promotion rates of FP students are higher than those for the university as a whole because of these factors. For example, in 1982, the FP promotion rate was 72 percent compared with 50 percent for all UNAN students. However, slightly more than one-fourth of FP students drop out or do not pass their examinations.

Steps have been taken by university leaders to place limits on the nonacademic activities of FP students. Such efforts are understandable in light of the intense nature of the program, the poor preparation of many of the entrants, and their multiple involvements in the tasks of the revolution, especially defense activities. In 1984, university officials requested of the national government that FP students not be subject to the draft.

Whether or not limitations on student military duty will remain in effect is uncertain. Also problematic is the extent to which greater emphasis will be placed on academic work. A more fundamental question concerns the extent to which the FP is a temporary program which will become obsolete as more working-class students complete secondary education through normal channels. At this point, no one has the answers.

Social Composition of Higher Education

Three factors which have contributed significantly to changing the social composition of higher education are an affirmative action policy designed to grant admission to students from disadvantaged regions and sectors of the society, the government commitment to free tuition for all higher-education students, and the establishment of the Preparatory Faculty. University education is no longer the exclusive preserve of elites. A substantial number of students from working-class and peasant backgrounds now have access to higher education, and within universities to the most prestigious faculties. Moreover, the number of women in higher education has grown to 44 percent of enrollments—not an ideal situation but an improvement over the 35 percent figure for 1977. This figure places Nicaragua alongside Costa Rica, the Dominican Republic, Venezuela, Chile, and Uruguay with 40 to 50 percent female enrollment figures, but below Panama and Argentina where women constitute a majority of higher-education students.

Although significant gains have been made in lower-class and minority enrollments, a majority of students still come from middle-class backgrounds. This is even more the case at UCA and within the National University system in such fields as medicine. A number of factors account for the failure of the present administration to radically alter the social class composition of the student body at higher levels of education. Limitations on financial aid mean that less than 15 percent of all students receive scholarships. Also, higher-education authorities have had to replace the open admission policy that pertained during the first year of the new government with a screening system that includes entrance examinations in mathematics, Spanish, and social studies, as well as ratings of academic performance during the last three semesters of secondary education, and student rankings of their career preferences. Such screening is necessary because the number of applicants exceeds the number of available higher-education places; this is particularly the case in priority areas with their more abundant scholarship opportunities, where there are at least two applicants for each place.

Not only are middle-class students advantaged in the competition, but similarly urban students fare better than their rural counterparts. To return to the example of the 550 entry slots available in the field of medicine, 370 were reserved for students from the Pacific Coast Zone, 150 for the North Central Zone, and 30 for the Atlantic Coast Zone. In the case of agronomic engineering, 25 of 600 positions are reserved for the Atlantic Coast. These lower figures are in accordance with the fact that about ten percent of the population resides in the region. The bulk of the population and a majority of secondary-school students are found in the Pacific Coast Region. In fact, 8,000 out of 15,000 secondary education graduates in 1984 came from the Managua area alone. These figures indicate past educational neglect of areas outside the main population centers of Managua, León, and Granada.

Since 1979, significant advances have been made in incorporating students from the most depressed region, but much more has to be accomplished before the social class composition of higher education, particularly the universities, is radically changed and adequate numbers are trained from regions such as the Atlantic Coast. The possibility of a regional university or campus for the Atlantic Coast, no matter how desirable, is a remote prospect, given the poverty of the country.

Within the university, it is conceded that faculties such as medicine and architecture are even more disproportionately middle class. Students in these selective fields have the additional advantage of being in a specialization where the promotion rate, once students are admitted, is significantly higher and where more resources are likely to be available. Medicine, for example, with 11 percent of higher education enrollments, receives approximately 15 percent of the budget. By contrast, students in less selective fields like economics comprise one-fifth of students and receive less than one-tenth of the higher education budget.

Women also suffer inequities in access to valued careers. Although more women are entering professional and nontraditional fields outside education, humanities, and nursing, general indications suggest they still are underrepresented in engineering, agricultural, and technological specializations.

Another effort to extend opportunity to the less advantaged and so change the social class composition of universities was attempted by UCA up until 1983, when it tried to institute a system of differential matriculation fees based on ability to pay. The scheme was abandoned either because the Sandinista government considered its commitment to the notion of free education at all levels to be inconsistent with a system of *quotas diferenciadas,* or because the government could not risk withdrawing the right of free tuition from the economic elites and middle class who are apprehensive over the social character of Sandinista policies.

While this response on the part of the government is understandable, the present system of free tuition, in effect, means that the state ends up subsidizing the costs of the more privileged groups in society to attend higher education institutions. Such are the constraints and contradictions of educational policies in a revolutionary situation.

Political Culture on Campus

It has long been the case that Latin American university students have been expected to be political actors and champions of popular social causes.[28] Historically, in the case of Nicaragua, student groups trace their origins back to the liberal, nationalist period of Benjamín Zeledón, and they commemorated the 70th anniversary of the university student movement on September 14, 1984. From the late 1950s on, university students and faculty were in the forefront of opposition to the Somoza family dictatorship. FSLN founders, Carlos Fonseca Amador, Tomás Borge, and Silvio Mayorga were student activists; and university students were the single most important source of FSLN organizers and combatants throughout much of the insurrectionary period.[29]

Since 1979, the constant mobilizations of youth for military service and participation in production brigades, as well as the intense politicization of many youths, have left their mark on higher education, and to a certain extent have transformed the university milieu. In many respects, there is a greater sense of purpose, a more profound seriousness, and even joy, in being a university student now than prior to the establishment of the new regime. During the final years of the Somoza dictatorship, it was considered a crime to be a youth, many students were arbitrarily and brutally victimized by the National Guard, and many youths turned to drugs as a form of escapism.[30] Compared to that period, the current spirit on campus is indeed upbeat. Festivities involving music and dance, fireworks, and a variety of high jinx (such as heaving students into the air or forming human pyramids) are associated with many of the mobilizations, along with the commemoration of the anniversaries of students who added their names to the long list of national martyrs.

The seriousness comes from being entrusted with significant responsibilities in constructing a new social order. Current student leaders claim that, unlike previous generations of student militants whose task was to oppose and destroy, their role is to construct and to promote. This assessment has merit. Moreover, student representatives are accorded key roles in departmental and university-wide decision making; and at the national level, through UNEN and JS–19 J, they have input into the highest consultative and policy councils shaping education.

The comingling of seriousness, commitment, and also guarded optimism about the future are expressed in the banners that abound on campuses proclaiming, for example, that if Nicaraguan youth are to enjoy their studies and be able to look forward to family life and satisfying careers, then they must fight for the survival of the revolutionary regime. Heroic efforts clearly are in demand if the country is to overcome decades of underdevelopment and if the current government is to prevail against a large-scale military invasion. Among those youth identifying with the FLSN, the most admired traits are those of "combativeness, enthusiasm, and revolutionary commitment."[31]

These themes are echoed in the campaigns of candidates for the top positions in the student centers. Napoleón López, who won the election for student body president of the UNAN/Managua-Rubén Darío campus in May 1984, ran on a platform calling for "strengthening of reserve battalions, support for production activities, revolutionary vigilance and civil defense."[32] His platform also called for improvement in the quality of teaching, stimulating student research, increasing the availability of learning materials, construction of school lunchrooms and bus shelters, and improvement of telephone services.[33]

UNEN, the mass organization that has replaced the vanguard JS–19 J in an effort to reach out and incorporate as many students into the revolutionary movement, actively promotes theater, music, poetry, and sports competitions. Extracurricular activities and intramural sports have never been so varied or important.

Altogether, it might be said that some 40, perhaps as much as 50 percent of the student body at places like UNAN/Managua are overtly involved with the Sandinista cause and display the traits of combativeness and revolutionary consciousness. Certainly no more than 25 percent belong to the more selective JS–19 J that has a mandatory screening period of six months. At least half the students could be characterized as neither committed to nor actively involved in revolutionary activities, with a small minority actively hostile. A number of shrewd observers allege that even among those who outwardly manifest a "militant" attitude, there are many who are opportunistically conforming and taking advantage of existing power alignments. Similarly, indifference may mask resentment or bitterness towards those in leadership positions.

As a case in point, the 6,000 UNAN/Managua students who participated in the cotton harvest of 1981, and the 5,000 who participated in the coffee harvest of 1982 were not merely manifesting revolutionary zeal, many were required to participate in order to fulfill their five-week work experience. What some resented was the fact that a number of the student leaders who exhorted them to go to the countryside were excused from these duties because of their organizational responsibilities in Managua. This may or may not have been the case, and abuse of privilege may have been minimal. The point is that even students sympathetic to the revolution believe there is something amiss in the universities.

The dark side of student commitment, involvement, and fervor is belligerence. According to some observers, this belligerence, coupled with intolerance, also distinguishes the current university milieu and has a deleterious effect on critical inquiry and dialogue. The intolerance is aimed at faculty and students who are not with the revolution or are considered hostile to it. Verbal abuse sometimes escalates into bullying and physical violence. Such abuses are not encouraged, nor are they condoned by the leadership of the FSLN. However, given the state of war in the country, outbursts of violence against ideologically opposed individuals and groups may be inevitable.

The effects of this situation, however, do not bode well for the university as one of the few places in the society where issues may be examined from different perspectives, and where government policies and actions, if erroneous, may be criticized. These concerns are expressed primarily not by opponents of the FSLN, but by highly-placed individuals in the government who have both an historical as well as ideal perspective on the Nicaraguan university system. Even during the worst days of the Somoza regime, students from different ideological backgrounds could openly debate value preferences, strategies, and tactics concerning deposing a common enemy and designing paths the society should take in the future. Unlike the 1970s when there was an active Christian socialist movement in UNAN and UCA, and alliances were formed between the Christian Revolutionary Movement (*Movimiento Cristiano Revolucionario*) and FSLN militants,[34] there is no such group active today on university campuses. Although the Conservative Democratic Party (*Partido Demócrata Cristiana,* PCD) and the extreme left parties have their youth wings, to date these groups have maintained a low profile and do not represent any serious challenge to the prevailing ideas of the Sandinista youth groups. Although there may be considerable conservative opposition off campus to the Sandinista government, there is, in effect, no such opposition in higher-education institutions.

One other component of the current ambience on campus is that of bureaucratization. The technocratic, manpower planning approach has been mentioned, as has the attempts by planning authorities to specify in detail the activities of students and faculty. This standardization requires a bureaucratic machinery. Not surprisingly, the number of administrative personnel increased by more than 50 percent between 1980–81 and 1983, from 1,153 to 1,827, as compared with a growth rate of only about 20 percent for faculty.[35]

Among administrative personnel there are a number of people loyal to the FSLN, but with few credentials or other qualifications for work in a university environment. Not unlike their colleagues in North American universities, they simply "follow orders." Their reluctance to make decisions, to even discuss the most routine affairs of their office or academic program areas without prior authorization of the rector's office, does not suggest an open intellectual or collegial environment. These are my own personal biases, which I forthrightly admit, because I find the bureaucratization of the university in North America no more desirable than in Nicaragua.

SUMMARY

The opening remarks of this chapter indicated that higher education was the most problematic level of the new Nicaraguan school system. This situation reflects past deficiencies of Nicaraguan higher education and extant problems in lower levels of schooling to which higher education is heir. But perhaps even more serious is the vision of the present FSLN educational leadership concerning what a more national and revolutionary higher-education system should look like. Post-1979 Nicaragua is not the first Latin American or Third World country to endeavor to envision and design a more indigenous system, one not modeled on that of a former colonial or hegemonic power.

Nicaragua most definitely has attempted to reject past North American influences on its university system. In rejecting one model, they have rushed to embrace another. The present Nicaraguan university, in many respects, is derivative of the Cuban model. Cuban influence is seen in many of the more significant changes in the higher education system and in curricular innovations. These innovations include greater emphasis on work-study experiences and the use of student assistants. The larger transformations include the planning of higher education policies (for enrollments, fellowships, fields of study, and faculty development) in close relation to human resource priorities; the elaboration of occupational profiles that serve as the guidelines for the design of five-year study plans specifying curricular content and activities—in effect the standardization of higher education in accordance with the decisions of central policy makers.

Fundamental questions concerning university autonomy, its nature and role, also have taken on a new hue. As in Cuba, it is argued that former liberal notions concerning university autonomy are romantic and no longer functional, that the antagonism that existed between the government and the people no longer obtains. The possibility now exists for the needs of the nation and the policies and programs of higher education institutions to mesh. Students and faculty, instead of using their energies and talents to oppose public policy, now have the opportunity to channel their knowledge and skills into the construction of a new society.

This point of view, however, is not unopposed. Among the positive aspects of the current situation is that debate still is possible concerning the direction of education, and what shape institutions should take. Some of the most highly-placed and respected educators argue against too narrow an economic definition of the role of the university. They strongly support the role of universities in fostering critical inquiry, and they favor the need for adequate political space so that debate and dialogue between differing points of view can take place. Moreover, they recognize that autonomy is absolutely necessary if higher education is to play the vital role of generating new knowledge.

Ultimately, the form and substance of Nicaraguan education will be shaped by the international context, the historical legacy, and the tensions and contradictions that are generated by the revolutionary process itself. In many respects, the end results are indeterminate and the process of change is still open-ended. What is more certain is that Nicaraguan higher education will be determined by Nicaraguans themselves in accordance with the realities of their situation.

NOTES

1. CNES, "Informe de la Gestión Julio 1979-May 1984," (Managua: *Consejo Nacional de la Educación Superior,* May 1984), p. 10.

2. MED, "Gestión Educativa," Table A–1. These figures of MED, however, do not accord with those in the above report by CNES.

3. CNES, "Informe Mayo 1984," p. 3.

4. Rolland G. Paulston and Fay Henderson Franklin, "U.S. Professors in Nicaraguan Universities: The LASPAU/AID Managua Project," (November 1983, mimeographed), p. 4.

5. Included in this list of former academics are Sergio Ramírez Mercado, current Vice-President and a former junta member; Fernando Cardenal, Minister of Education; Carlos Tünnermann Bernheim, former Minister of Education and current Ambassador to the United States; and Bayardo Arce who is a member of the National Directorate of the FSLN.

6. CNES, "Informe Mayo 1984," p. 16.

7. CNES, "Programa de 1984," (Managua: *Consejo Nacional de la Educación Superior, Dirección de Planificación,* 1984), p. 18 passim.

8. Oswaldo Chávez Arévalo, "Francisco Espinoza . . . Panchon Presente" (June 1984), p. 3. Academic Vice-Rector's Office, UNAN/Managua-Rubén Darío campus.

9. Interview with William Genet, CNES, Managua, May 18, 1984.

10. See, for example, Robert F. Arnove, "Foundations and the Transfer of Knowledge," in his edited collection, *Philanthropy and Cultural Imperialism*

(Boston: G.K. Hall, 1980), pp. 305–30.

11. Interview with the Rector of UCA, Miguel Angel Ruiz, Managua, May 23, 1984.

12. CNES, "Informe Mayo 1984," p. 16.

13. Ibid., pp. 15–16.

14. See, for example, Paulston and Henderson Franklin," LASPAU Project."

15. Miguel de Castilla Urbina, *Educación y Lucha de Clases en Nicaragua* (Managua: Departamento de Filosofía, Universidad Centro Americana, 1980), pp. 98–134 passim.

16. CNES, "Informe de Mayo 1984," p. 1.

17. Whether or not the upper levels of engineering education will be completely phased out of UNAN and UCA was being reconsidered in late 1984.

18. For critiques of the manpower planning approach see Mark Blaug, *An Introduction to the Economics of Education* (Middlesex, England: Penguin Books, 1972), chapter on "The Manpower Requirements Approach," pp. 137–68; and his "The Empirical Status of Human Capital Theory: A Slightly Jaundiced Survey," *Journal of Economic Literature* 14 (September 1975): 827–55. Also see Irvin Sobel, "The Human Capital Revolution in Economic Development," *Comparative Education Review* 22 (June 1978): 267–308.

19. Michael E. Conroy, "False Polarisation? Differing Perspectives on the Economic Strategies of Post-Revolutionary Nicaragua," *Third World Quarterly* 6 (October 1984): 993–1032.

20. CNES, "Informe Mayo 1984," p. 12.

21. Ibid., pp. 19–21.

22. William Genet, "Transformación Curricular," (CNES, mimeographed, n.d.).

23. See, for example, Paulston and Henderson Franklin, "LASPAU Project," p. 28.

24. Information in this paragraph was provided by American physician Jan Diamond, Managua, June 2, 1984.

25. During this period, three medical students were killed. See "Estudiantes de Medicina hacia las Zonas de Combate," *Barricada,* June 1, 1984, p. 10.

26. Ibid., interview with medical student Bismarck Valverde.

27. Interview with Oswaldo Chávez Arévalo, Academic Vice-Rector, UNAN/Managua-Rubén Darío Campus, June 11, 1984.

28. See, for example, Robert F. Arnove, "A Survey of Literature and Research on Latin American Universities," *Latin American Research Review* 3 (Fall 1967): 45–62; and Robert F. Arnove chapter, "Students in Politics" in *Venezuela: The Democratic Experience,* John D. Martz and David Meyer, ed. (New York: Praeger, 1977), pp. 195–214.

29. See Nolan, *FSLN*; and Castilla, *Lucha de Clases,* esp. pp. 113–20.

30. According to many observers of the university scene in the pre-1979 period, the National Guard was the main distributor of drugs on university campuses. Drugs were a source of income for corrupt guardsmen and one means of diverting students from politics.

31. "Retroguardia de Jovenes Dispuestos a Combatir," *Barricada,* May 26, 1984, p. 8.

32. "Comienzan Hoy Elecciones Universitarias," *El Nuevo Diario,* May 10, 1984, p. 9.

33. Ibid.

34. Nolan, *FSLN,* pp. 51–2.

35. Mariano Vargas Narváez, "Situación Socio-Económico y Educación Superior Antes y Después del Triunfo de la Revolución Popular Sandinista," (CNES, mimeographed, May 1983), p. 38; and MED, "Gestión Educativa Mayo 1984," Table A–1.

6
Conclusions

Education has been called upon to play a key role in the revolutionary changes in Nicaragua since 1979. According to the MED:

> Since the triumph of the Popular Sandinista Revolution, the Ministry of Education has given Education *a single direction*: the transformation of the entire education system—its organization, structure, curriculum, plans and programs, its methodology, texts, teachers. . . .
>
>   This direction corresponded to a single imperative: to make education a coherent reality with the Revolution.[1]

Toward that end, the Nicaraguan education system has expanded dramatically, and measures have been taken to improve the quality of teaching and change the content of instruction as well as to transform the social relations of learning.

In quantitative terms, the achievements of the past five years include a literacy campaign that taught over 406,000 people to read and write, lowering the illiteracy rate from 50.3 percent to under 15 percent; the establishment of a program of ongoing adult basic education, staffed by over 20,000 volunteer teachers that reaches approximately 200,000 Nicaraguans; the doubling of formal school enrollments from 501,660 students in 1978 to 1,127,428 in 1984. Altogether, over one-third (38 percent) of the Nicaraguan population was enrolled in some form of publicly-supported systematic instruction in 1984.[2]

The expansion of educational services has been made possible by more than quadrupling the education budget from approximately 400 million cordobas in 1979 to over 1.7 billion cordobas in 1984 (representing nearly 4.9 percent of gross domestic product) and by dramatically expanding the teaching force from 12,706 in 1978 to 53,398 (in both formal and nonformal education) by 1984.[3] The increased allocations have led to the construction of schools in previously neglected rural areas of the country as well as to the addition of school libraries, laboratories, and workshops to existing facilities. The expansion of the teaching force has been accompanied by a program of systematic inservice upgrading and by steps to improve the status and working conditions of teachers. Work loads have been reduced by one-fifth while salaries, in 1984, were increased by 50 to 100 percent.

Among the major improvements in schooling have been the establishment of a national textbook industry, the revision of curricula, and the introduction of new methods of instruction, particularly in the language arts. Organizationally, while the Ministry of Education in Managua plays a more central role in long-range planning and in the formulation of more coherent policies for the entire system, there has been a significant decentralization and regionalization of administrative services, including greater cultural autonomy for the Atlantic Coast zones in educational programming.

Transformations in learning center on fostering more collective, participatory, inquiry-oriented and work-related methods. Major steps have been taken to involve the schools more directly in the activities of their surrounding communities and in the resolution of national problems. Rural Educational Núcleos (NER), for example, represent a significant attempt to employ rural school networks as a vehicle for bringing together state agencies, mass organizations, and school personnel for community development purposes. At the higher education level, the most striking transformations involve the close integration of admissions policies and faculty and curriculum development with national economic plans, and the inclusion of a significant work component in all study plans.

The leadership of the MED envision the expansion, improvement, and transformation of education as, respectively, contributing to the democratization of basic social services, the independence of the Nicaraguan economy from foreign domination, and the development of a new model of capital accumulation based on different social relations of production and new forms of public and cooperative ownership. The overriding goal of education has been to "contribute to the formation of the new man [and woman] and the new society."[4]

These are lofty ideals, indeed. It would be totally unprecedented if the Nicaraguan education system, in the brief period of five years, were able to make a substantial contribution to achieving these goals. The experience of other revolutionary societies indicate that change in school systems typically lags behind economic and political changes; the recruitment and training of teachers and the revision of curriculum takes years, and does not always lead to the desired outcomes.[5] The schooling process itself usually involves a minimum of nine years to provide both a basic education and rudimentary technical/vocational skills. In the meantime, society is in upheaval, with pressing demands to be satisfied.

Yet, in many ways, the post-1979 educational program and activities of the Sandinista government have contributed significantly to the consolidation of the new regime and to its plans for social and economic change. The singular most successful educational activity to date—the national literacy crusade—conferred, both symbolically and substantively, citizenship rights on previously excluded segments of the society and constituted the first step in the political mobilization of large numbers of youths and adults. It further contributed to the integration of countryside and city, Atlantic and Pacific Coasts of the country, and to the strengthening of mass organizations and their role in national reconstruction. The literacy campaign and the follow-up program of adult popular education have imparted skills and knowledge, and have altered self-perceptions of previously excluded peasants, workers, and women, who are not only putting their recently acquired knowledge to work in new productive and political roles, but are acquiring further education to more adequately meet the daily challenges they confront. At the other end of the spectrum, higher education institutions have graduated over 7,000 professionals and technicians who are extending the provision of basic social services and contributing to the modernization of the economy.

Whether or not a new Nicaraguan person has been forged by the education system is questionable. The experiences of the USSR, China, Cuba, and Tanzania suggest that transformation in the political culture of a society, let alone the school system, is not easily wrought. The political content of instruction may change, but old attitudes, beliefs, and behaviors may not. The education system may provide more opportunities to behave in new ways, but the greatest socializing impact on system-relevant values and conduct is more likely to be effected by the revolutionary changes in society itself, by the demands placed on youths by structurally altered circumstances. As Fagen has noted with regard to Cuba, the constant mobilizations of a revolutionary society may require people to act in new ways, even though their attitudes, initially, may not be congruent with the new roles they play.[6] Certainly, the continuation of the good will engendered by the literacy campaign and the provision of basic education to the populace at large is contingent upon the continuing efforts of the Sandinista government to satisfy people's aspirations for improvements in their life circumstances. Similarly, political lessons taught in school, but not reinforced outside the classroom in daily life, are unlikely to take hold.

Nicaragua offers an illustration of the reciprocal nature of the relationship between school and society: education not only influences development but is contingent upon it.[7] In the case of Nicaragua, the revolutionary environment, while providing opportunities for the acquisition of new skills and the utilization of knowledge for collective ends, also places serious limitations on the educational enterprise. These constraints stem from the poverty of the country, its legacy of underdevelopment, and its strategic position within the U.S. sphere of influence. The current mobilizations to raise production and defend the country against external aggression have a powerful socializing impact: they are palpable lessons in Nicaraguan history and geography, political economy, and international relations. The mobilizations, however, also disrupt the schooling process, making it more difficult for students to acquire the knowledge and skills relevant to the attainment of Nicaragua's economic goals. The war situation means that allocations to education and other social services must be curtailed. The role of education in social change further means that schools and teachers are singled out for attack by counterrevolutionaries.

In his five-year summary report, Minister of Education Carlos Tünnermann Bernheim noted both the promise and limitations of education's contribution to the revolution, as well as some of the contradictions that surround education.

> It is not possible . . . to conceive of a revolutionary process without a transformation, at base, in the education system. . . . But with regard to this point, I do not wish to say that Education ought to change brusquely overnight.[8]
>
> The Education System responds to the rhythm of political-economic transformations that emanate from the revolutionary philosophy . . . but does not generate them because its superstructural condition does not permit it to do so. . . . Similarly, with development: it [education] is not a determining cause, but it can promote or retard it.[9]

From a Marxist point of view, education may form part of the cultural and intellectual superstructure of society determined by the economic base, but Marx himself noted, "The materialist doctrine that men are products of circumstances and upbringing, and that, therefore, changed men are products of other circumstances and changed upbringing, forgets that it is men that change circumstances and the educator himself needs educating.[10]

While the Nicaraguan education system is shaped to a great extent by economic forces and is the object of political control by the National Directorate of the FSLN, it also has a good deal of autonomy. This has been the case in other socialist countries where the state has attempted, according to Fagerlind and Saha, to "harness the educational system in the attainment" of objects related to the creation of a collectively- and achievement-oriented person and rapid development.[11]

The refractory and intractable nature of formal school systems is particularly evident in Nicaragua. Over and beyond the autonomy that characterizes education as a subsystem of the society, there has been considerable debate within the political leadership of the FSLN, and among MED personnel, different state agencies, and the mass organizations (such as ANDEN and JS–19 J) over educational policy. Education is often contrasted with the field of health. In health care the goals are clear; what people disagree over is the best way to deliver health services or achieve an agreed upon objective. By comparison, what constitutes good education or the desired end-state is not clear, nor is there agreement over the means to achieve goals agreed upon.

One of the key debates concerns the emphasis within current educational policy on the formal school system as against nonformal education. Former Vice-Minister of Education Miguel de Castilla Urbina, for example, has pointed out the paradox of depending on a system that for 100 years has, as an instrument of elite domination, been preparing a fragmented and obedient workforce, rather than relying more on popular (out-of-school) education programs that derive from a revolutionary heritage and that are aimed at liberating people.[12]

Other debates have centered on the proper balance between academics and politics, on the emphasis to be given to developing expertise as against raising consciousness.[13] Related issues have included the relationship between general and technical education; the extent to which advanced technical training should be offered within the country or sought abroad; and the amount of autonomy to be granted universities.

These are debates within the political and educational leadership of the FSLN. Generally, within Nicaraguan society, and especially on the part of those individuals and groups opposed to the current regime, there is considerable disagreement over the content of political and civics instruction and the degree of public control over private education. But even the Sandinista leadership is not ideologically unified, nor in total accord on the pace and scope of social change and on the political content of education.

As previous chapters in this book have indicated, the issues facing educators are not easily resolved. To return to the debate over formal versus nonformal education, among the difficulties faced in relying on formal schooling to effect change is the poor preparation of teachers and, often, their lack of political commitment.[14] The volunteer teachers in adult popular education programs (EPB) tend to be more politically militant, but they are even more poorly prepared. And notwithstanding expectations and rhetoric on the part of advocates of EPB, they are unlikely to implement innovative pedagogical methods based on dialogue and consciousness raising. Furthermore, as Chapter 3 indicated, adult basic education has become increasingly bureaucratic and lethargic over time, and pervaded by a schooling ideology, with many of the youths who enter EPB endeavoring to use nonformal educational programs to gain access to formal schooling and advanced credentials. The participatory aspects of popular education programs that take place in the workplace and community, and by means of adult education, also are frequently characterized by top-down control and unreflective transmission of political messages from organizational leaders and ultimately the National Directorate of the FSLN.

The proper balance between political socialization and cognitive development has proven to be an elusive goal and a source of considerable ideological debate in all revolutionary socialist societies. In the case of Nicaragua, the evidence suggests that primary education, as well as adult basic education, has been more heavily weighted on the side of political education rather than on skill development. At the secondary level, however, education may be overly academic and geared toward university preparation. At the tertiary level, education has been too narrowly specialized, vocational and technical, not conforming to Marxist notions of a broad, "polytechnic" formation.[15]

It is not unusual that Nicaragua should experience these problems during the first five years of its revolution. Cuba, for example, reported similar problems some 12 years after its revolution. In 1971, these problems included a majority of the teaching force (73 percent) poorly prepared and uncertified; high dropout and repeater rates in primary education; a disproportionate number of students enrolled in general education at the secondary level; and within technical education, insufficient enrollment in agricultural fields.[16]

These problems were not remedied until a restructuring of the education system took place in the mid-1970s, when the decision was made to provide a general polytechnical education of nine years to all students that would lead to specialized technical-vocational training for most (grades 10–12) or preuniversity education for a few. By 1980, 20 years after the initiation of the revolution, the Cuban education system had begun to conform to the vision of the political and educational leadership of the country. In China and the USSR, educational policies have taken dramatic swings to accord with changes in political leadership; and in the case of China, its education system, again, is undergoing reorganization and shifts in emphasis.[17]

The reconstruction of the Nicaraguan education system is only just beginning. A new direction has been articulated to make education a coherent reality with the revolution, but many of the announced reforms still exist largely on paper. It may be that with more time and with the consolidation of the present political regime, Nicaragua will be able to fulfill tangible—and modest—goals such as providing a minimum of four years of basic education to its entire population, ensuring that no school child has to sit on a mud floor, and that every student has textbooks. With time and resources, it is possible that a basic education of 9 or 12 years will be available to every Nicaraguan youth, and that an education will be in place that develops the talents of individuals and also satisfies the economic requirements of the country.

But time, resources, and political latitude are precisely the factors and conditions that are not now available, for the Sandinista government is presently involved in a life and death struggle that will determine its own survival and whether or not the revolution will continue along the trajectory demarcated in 1979. Once again, the United States, which at various times in the past either occupied or indirectly ruled the country through surrogates,[18] has decided that Nicaragua, an impoverished country of 3 million, represents a direct threat to its hegemonic and security interests in Central America and the Caribbean. To a great extent, the fate not just of education but of all Nicaraguan institutions is being determined by policy formulated in Washington, D.C., where the executive and legislative branches of government have supported invasions by counterrevolutionary forces and an economic war that denies Nicaragua markets, capital, and materials.

The United States attempts to justify its position vis-à-vis Nicaragua by labelling the Sandinista government a "Marxist-Leninist dictatorship" heavily influenced by the Soviet model. In reality, the present situation in Nicaragua defies facile categorization. The post-1979 social experiment there is unique.

While the new Nicaraguan leadership attempts to pursue its own path to development, learning from its past and the experiences of other countries, East and West, it is important for outsiders to develop a more judicious perspective. The complexity and open-endedness of the revolutionary processes occurring in Nicaragua require that observers not rush to quick generalizations or point to Nicaragua as a model to be emulated by other countries. The situation also requires that other countries not try to impose their will, models, and ideas on Nicaragua—a recurring theme throughout that society's tumultuous history. Political action is one path for those committed to self-determination for Nicaragua. Scholarship may contribute, as well, to the ideal of self-determination. In this respect, the task of scholarship is to conduct the kind of inquiry that places problems in context and exposes contradictions that need to be transcended if the government is to reach the goals it has set for itself. It is hoped that this study has illuminated the potential and limitations of one key institution to contribute to the social transformations occurring in revolutionary Nicaragua.

NOTES

1. MED, *Política y Lineamientos,* p. 6.
2. Figures on the accomplishments of the Nicaraguan education system are summarized in Tünnermann, "Cinco Años de Eduación; and MED, "Gestión Educativa Cinco Años," especially Tables A–1 to A–6.
3. Ibid.

4. MED, *Consulta Nacional,* p. 139.

5. On teachers, for example, see Miguel de Castilla Urbina, "La Educación como Poder, Crisis sin Solución en la Transición Revolucionaria: El Caso de Nicaragua 1978–1981," paper presented to the Second Nicaraguan Social Sciences Congress, Managua, August 21–23, 1981, pp. 64–68; on curriculum change, see his, "La Contradicción Contenidos de la Educación y Contenidos de la Revolución: Una Propuesta de Solución," paper presented to the Third Nicaraguan Social Sciences Congress, Managua, October 29–31, 1982.

6. Fagen, *Transformation of Political Culture,* pp. 151–55.

7. See Ingemar Fägerlind and Lawrence J. Saha, *Education and National Development: A Comparative Perspective* (New York: Pergamon Press, 1983), p. 195.

8. Tünnermann, "Cinco Años de Educación," p. 1.

9. Ibid., p. 2.

10. Karl Marx, "Theses on Feuerbach: III", in *Karl Marx and Frederick Engels: Selected Works* (London: Lawrence & Wisehart, 1968 (1888), p. 28; cited in Fägerlind and Saha, *Education and Development,* p. 224.

11. Fägerlind and Saha, *Education and Development,* p. 248.

12. Castilla de Urbina, "Educación Como Poder," p. 53.

13. On the pendular swings in emphasis on expertise and political consciousness in China, see Theodore Hsi-en Chen, *Chinese Education Since 1949: Academic and Revolutionary Models* (New York: Pergamon, 1982).

14. Miguel de Castilla, "Educación Como Poder," pp. 64–68.

15. For further discussion, see Fägerlind and Saha, *Education and Development,* p. 226.

16. "Educación en Cuba, Informe Presentado por la Delegación Cubana a la Conferencia de Ministros de Educación de América Latina," Mexico City, December 1976, pp. 9–11.

17. John F. Burns, "China Orders Changes in Its Educational Policies," *New York Times,* June 2, 1985, p. 5; for an analysis of recent trends in Chinese education, see Stanley Rosen, "Recentralization, Decentralization and Rationalization: Deng Xiaoping's Bifurcated Educational Policy," *Modern China* (July 1985).

18. For a discussion of U.S. intervention in Nicaragua, see LaFeber, *Inevitable Revolutions,* pp. 11, 46–48, 226–41, 293–98; and Walker, *Land of Sandino,* esp. chaps. 1 and 7.

Bibliography

Academy for Educational Development, *Nicaraguan Education Sector Assessment.* Managua and Washington, D.C.: AED, 1975.

Altbach, Philip G., Robert F. Arnove, and Gail P. Kelly, eds. *Comparative Education.* New York: Macmillan, 1982.

Apple, Michael. *Education and Power.* London: Routledge & Kegan Paul, 1982.

Arnove, Robert F. "A Survey of Literature and Research on Latin American Universities," *Latin American Research Review* 3 (Fall 1967): 45–62.

_____. "A View from Nicaragua: Literacy Campaigns and the Transformation of Political Culture." In *Latin America and Caribbean Contemporary Record,* Vol. 2, 1982–83, edited by Jack W. Hopkins, pp. 245–60. New York: Holmes & Meier, 1984.

_____. "Foundations and the Transfer of Knowledge." In *Philanthropy and Cultural Imperialism: The Foundations at Home and Abroad,* edited by Robert F. Arnove, pp. 305–30. Boston: G.K. Hall, 1980.

_____. "The Nicaraguan National Literacy Crusade of 1980." *Comparative Education Review* 25 (June 1981): 244–59.

_____. "Students in Politics." In *Venezuela: The Democratic Experience,* edited by John D. Martz and David Meyer, pp. 195–214. New York: Praeger, 1977.

Arnove, Robert F. and Jairo Arboleda, "Literacy: Power or Mystification?" *Literacy Discussion* 4 (December 1973): 389–414.

Arnove, Robert F., Michael Chiappetta, and Sylvia Stalker, "Latin American Education." In *Latin America and Caribbean Contemporary Record,* edited by Jack W. Hopkins. New York: Holmes & Meier, 1986.

Arríen, Juan Bautista. *Nicaragua: Revolución y Proyecto Educativo.* Managua: Ministry of Education, 1980.

Asociación de Mujeres Nicaragüenses "Luisa Amanda Espinoza" (AMNLAE). "Women's Participation in the New Nicaragua." *Contemporary Marxism* 8 (Spring 1984): 122–28.

Barndt, Deborah. "Popular Education." In *Nicaragua: The First Five Years,* edited by Thomas W. Walker, pp. 317–46. New York: Praeger, 1985.

Bernardo, Robert M. "Moral Stimulation as a Non-Market Mode of Labor Allocation in Cuba." *Studies in Comparative International Development,* vol. 6, no. 6 (1970–71): 119–38.

Bhola, H.S. *Campaigning for Literacy.* Paris: UNESCO, 1982.

Blaug, Mark. *An Introduction to the Economics of Education.* Middlesex, England: Penguin Books, 1972.

_____. The Empirical status of Human Capital Theory: A Slightly Jaundiced Survey." *Journal of Economic Literature* 14 (September 1976): 827–55.

Bock, John C. "Education and Development: A Conflict of Meanings." In *Comparative Education,* edited by Philip G. Altbach, Robert F. Arnove, and Gail P. Kelly, pp. 78–101. New York: Macmillan, 1982.

Boocock, Sarane S. *An Introduction to the Sociology of Learning,* 2nd ed., New York: Houghton Mifflin, 1982.

Borge, Tomás et al. *Sandinistas Speak.* New York: Pathfinder Press, 1982.

Bourdieu, Pierre and J.C. Passerow. *Reproduction.* Beverly Hills, CA: Sage, 1977.

Bourgois, Philippe. "Class, Ethnicity and the State among the Miskito Amerindians of Northeastern Nicaragua." *Latin American Perspectives* 29 (Spring 1981): 22–39.

_____. "Nicaragua's Ethnic Minorities in the Revolution." *Monthly Review* 37 (January 1985): 22–4.

Bowles, Samuel. "Cuban Education and the Revolutionary Ideology." *Harvard Educational Review* 41 (November 1971): 472–500.

Burns, John F. "China Orders Changes in Its Educational Policies." *New York Times,* June 2, 1985, p. 5.

Bustamante, Homero. "A Summary History of Thirty-Five Years of U.S. Government Cooperation in Nicaraguan Socio-Economic Development." Nicaragua: United States Agency for International Development, United States Embassy, January 1978. Mimeographed.

Cabezas, Omar. *Fire from the Mountain.* New York: Crown, 1985.

Cardenal, Fernando and Valerie Miller, "Nicaragua 1980: The Battle of the ABCs." *Harvard Educational Review* 51 (February 1981): 1–26.

Carnoy, Martin. *Education as Cultural Imperialism.* New York: David McKay, 1974.

Chávez Arévalo, Oswaldo. "*Francisco Espinoza . . . Panchon Presente.*" Managua: Academic Vice-Rector's Office, UNAN/Rubén Darío campus. Mimeographed.

Chen, Theodore Hsi-en. *Chinese Education since 1949: Academic and Revolutionary Models.* New York: Pergamon, 1982.

Coleman, James S. *The Adolescent Society.* New York: Free Press, 1961.

Collins, Joseph et al. *Nicaragua: What Difference Could a Revolution Make?,* 2nd ed. San Francisco: Institute for Food and Development Policy, 1985.

"Comienzan Hoy Elecciones Universitarias." *El Nuevo Diario,* May 10, 1984, p. 9.

CNES, National Higher Education Council. "Informe de la Gestión Julio 1979-Mayo 1984." Managua: CNES, May 1984. Mimeographed.

_____. "Programa de 1984." Managua: Department of Planning/CNES, 1984. Mimeographed.

Conroy, Michael E. "False Polarisation? Differing Perspectives on the Economic Strategies of Post-Revolutionary Nicaragua." *Third World Quarterly* 6 (October 1984): 993–1032.

Crahan, Margaret E. "Varieties of Faith: Religion in Contemporary Nicaragua." Working paper No. 5, Occidental College, December 1983. Mimeographed.

De Castilla Urbina, Miguel. "La Contradicción Contenidos de la Educación y Contenidos de la Revolución: Una Propuesta de Solución." Paper presented to the Third Nicaraguan Social Studies Congress, Managua, October 29–31, 1982. Mimeographed.

_____. "La Educación como Poder, Crisis sin Solución en la Transición Revolucionaria: El Caso de Nicaragua 1978–81." Paper presented to the Second Nicaraguan Social Sciences Congress, Managua, August 21–23. Mimeographed.

_____. La Educación en Nicaragua: Un Caso de Educación para el Desarrollo de Subdesarrollo. Managua: Institute for Human Promotion, INPRHU, 1976.

_____. Educación y Lucha de Clases en Nicaragua. Managua: Philosophy Department, Central American University, 1980.

Dennis, Philip A. "The Costeños and the Revolution in Nicaragua." *Journal of Interamerican Studies and World Affairs,* 23 (August 1981): 271–96.

Departamento Ecuménico de Investigaciones, Ecumenical Research Department. *Nicaragua Triunfa en la Alfabetización,* compiled and edited by Hugo Assmann. San José, Costa Rica: DEI, and Managua: Ministry of Education, 1981.

Dreeben, Robert. *On What Is Learned in School.* Reading, Mass.: Addison Wesley, 1968.

Dussel, Enrique. *Theology of Liberation.* Maryknoll, N.Y.: Orbis Books, 1976.

"Educación en Cuba." Paper presented by the Cuban Delegation at the Conference of Latin American Ministers of Education, Mexico City, December 1979.

English, Deirdre. "We Are Sandinistas: Conversations with Nicaragua's Embattled Leaders." *Mother Jones,* August/September 1985, pp. 22–28, 51.

"Estudiantes Cristianos para la Defensa." *El Nuevo Diario,* June 20, 1984.

"Estudiantes de Medicina hacia las Zonas de Combate." *Barricada,* June 1, 1984, p. 10.

Fagen, Richard, *The Transformation of Political Culture in Cuba.* Stanford: Stanford University Press, 1969.

Fägerlind, Ingemar and Lawrence J. Saha. *Education and National Development: A Comparative Perspective.* New York: Pergamon, 1983.

Flora, Jan L., John McFadden, and Ruth Warner. "The Growth of Class Struggle: The Impact of the Nicaraguan Literacy Crusade on the Political Consciousness of Young Literacy Workers." *Latin American Perspectives* 36 (Winter 1983): 45–61.

Freire, Paulo. "The Adult Education Process as Cultural Action for Freedom." *Harvard Educational Review* 40 (May 1970): 205–23.

_____. *Pedagogy of the Oppressed.* New York: Herder and Herder, 1970.

FSLN Dirreción Nacional. "Why the FSLN Struggles in Unity with the People." *Latin American Perspectives.* 20 (Winter 1970): 108–13.

_____. *Participatory Democracy.* Managua: the same, 1984.

Geffre, Claude and Gustavo Gutiérrez, eds. *The Mystical and Political Dimension of the Christian Faith.* New York: Herder and Herder, 1974.

Genet, William. "Transformación Curricular." Managua: National Higher Education Council, CNES, n.d.

Gillette, Arthur. *Cuba's Educational Revolution.* London: Fabian Society, 1972.

Giroux, Henry. *Ideology, Culture and the Process of Schooling.* Philadelphia: Temple University Press, 1984.

Gorostiaga, Xavier. "Dilemmas of the Nicaraguan Revolution." In *The Future of Central America,* edited by Richard Fagen and Olga Pellicer, pp. 47–66. Stanford: Stanford University Press, 1983.

Goulet, Denis. *A New Moral Order: Development Ethics and Liberation Theology.* Maryknoll, N.Y.: Orbis Books, 1974.

Guevara, Onofre. "La JS 19: Una Posición Ganada en la Lucha." *Barricada,* December 22, 1981, p. 3.

Hershon, Sheryl with Judy Butler. *And Also Teach Them to Read.* Westport, Conn.: Lawrence Hill, 1983.

Habed López, Jader and Mario Trana Matus. *La Educación en Nicaragua.* Managua: Division of Human Resources, Ministry of Public Education, 1964.

Halperin, David C. and Richard Garfield. "Developments in Health Care in Nicaragua," *New England Journal of Medicine,* 307 (1982): 388–92.

Hoge, Warren, "Women Win New Role in Nicaragua." *Austin American Statesman,* January 15, 1981, p. E–4.

"The Impact of Civil War in Nicaragua." Washington, D.C.: Center for International Policy, n.d. Mimeographed "Fact Sheet."

Jung, Harald. "Behind the Nicaraguan Revolution." *New Left Review,* no. 117 (September-October 1979): 69–89.

Karabel, Jerome and A.H. Halsey, "Educational Research: A Review and Interpretation." In *Power and Ideology in Education,* edited by Jerome Karabel and A.H. Halsey, pp. 1–86. New York: Oxford University Press, 1977.

Kaspar, Jan, ed., *Nicaragua for the Eradication of Illiteracy.* Paris: International Union of Students and UNESCO, n.d.

Kelly, Gail P., Philip G. Altbach, and Robert F. Arnove. "Trends in Comparative Education: A Critical Analysis." In *Comparative Education,* edited by Philip

Key, V.O., Jr. *Public Opinion and American Democracy.* New York: Knopf, 1961.

Kozol, Jonathan. "A New Look at the Literacy Campaign in Cuba." *Harvard Educational Review* 48 (Summer 1978): 341–77.

Kraft, Richard J. "Global Survival: Nicaragua." In *Foundations of Education: Social Perspectives* by Richard D. Van Scotter, Richard J. Kraft, and John D. Hass, pp. 355–62. Englewood Cliffs, N.J.: Prentice-Hall, 1979.

_____. "Nicaragua: Educational Opportunity under Pre- and Post-Revolutionary Conditions." In *Politics and Education: Cases from Eleven Nations,* edited by Murray Thomas, pp. 79–103. New York: Pergamon, 1983.

Lacayo, Francisco. Speech. In *Primer Congreso Nacional de Educación Popular de Adultos: Documentos, pp. 33–38. Managua: Ministry of Education, June 1981.*

LaFeber, Walter. *Inevitable Revolutions: The United States and Central America.* New York: W.W. Norton, 1983.

Landsberger, Harry A., ed. The Church and Social Change in Latin America. Notre Dame, Ind.: University of Notre Dame Press, 1970.

Leiken, Robert. "Nicaragua's Untold Story." *New Republic,* October 8, 1984, pp. 16–22.

LeoGrande, M. William. "The United States and Nicaragua." In *Nicaragua: The First Five Years,* edited by Thomas W. Walker, pp. 425–47. New York: Praeger, 1985.

Macías Gómez, Edgar. "Análisis de la Estructura y Funcionamiento del Sistema Nacional de Educación de Adultos." In *Educación y Dependencía,* edited by Instituto de Promoción Humana. Managua: Nicaragua, Institute for Human Promotion, INPRHU, 1976.

_____. Alfabetización de Adultos Nicaragüenses. Managua: INPRHU, 1972.

Mikkonen, Anita. "The Literacy Crusade and the Children." In *Nicaragua for the Eradication of Illiteracy,* edited by Jan Kaspar. Paris: International Union of Students and UNESCO, n.d.

Millett, Richard. *Guardians of the Dynasty: A History of the U.S. Created Guardia Nacional de Nicaragua and the Somoza Family.* Maryknoll, N.Y.: Orbis Books, 1977.

Miller, Valerie. *Between Struggle and Hope: The Nicaraguan Literacy Crusade.* Boulder, Col.: Westview Press, 1985.

_____. "The Nicaraguan Literacy Crusade." In *Nicaragua in Revolution,* edited by Thomas W. Walker, pp. 241–58. New York: Praeger, 1982.

Minano García, Max H. *Proyecto Piloto de Educación Fundamental del Río Coco.* Managua: Ministry of Public Education, 1960.

Ministry of Education. *Consulta Nacional para Obtener Criterios que Ayuden a Definir los Fines y Objetivos de la Educación Nicaragüense, Informe Preliminar.* Managua: MED, August 1981.

_____. *La Cruzada en Marcha.* Bulletin No. 13. Managua: National Literacy Crusade, CNA/MED, July 1980.

_____. "IV Jornada Estudiantil de Ciencia y Producción Augusto C. Sandino." Managua: Department of Secondary Education/MED, 1984. Mimeographed.

_____. "La Gestión Educativa en Cinco Años de Revolución." Managua: MED, May 1984.

_____. "The Great National Literacy Campaign: Heroes and Martyrs for the Creation of Nicaragua." Managua: MED, January 1980; translated and edited by the National Network in Solidarity with the Nicaraguan People, Washington, D.C. Mimeographed.

_____. "Líneas Principales de la Política Educativa del Ministerio de Educación para 1984." Managua: MED, 1984. Mimeographed.

_____. "La Nuclearización Educativa Nicaragüense en el Contexto de la Revolución Popular Sandinista." Managua: Department of Educational Nuclearization/MED, September 1984. Mimeographed.

_____. "Orientaciones Generales para Lograr la Participación de los Alumnos en Tareas Socialmente Utiles y el Cuidado de la Propiedad Social." Department of Primary Education/MED, June 1984. Mimeographed.

_____. "Para Estructurar un Núcleo Educativo Rural." Managua: Department of Nuclearization/MED, March 1984. Mimeographed.

_____. *Plan Nacional de Acción de Nicaragua en el Marco del Proyecto Principal de Educación.* Managua: MED, 1982.

_____. "Plan Operativo para Estructurar el Modelo de Participación Popular: Propuesta." Managua: Department of Educational Nuclearization/MED, March 1984. Mimeographed.

_____. "Política y Lineamientos del Desarrollo Educativo dentro del Plan Nacional de Desarrollo de la Educación No Superior de Nicaragua a Mediano Plazo (1984–1990). Managua: General Division of Planning/MED, 1983.

_____. *Primer Congreso Nacional de Educación Popular de Adultos: Documentos.* Managua: MED, June 6-7, 1981.

_____. *Proposiciones para Establecer la Filosofía, los Objetivos, las Líneas de Acción y la Estructura de la 'EPA' en Nicaragua para Contribuir al Proceso de la Reconstrucción Nacional.* Managua: MED, July 1979.

_____. "Proyecto de Educación Bilingüe-Bicultural: Plan de Trabajo Junio-Diciembre 1984." Special Zone 1/MED, May 21, 1984. Mimeographed.

Ministry of Health. "Jornadas Populares de Salud" Managua: MINSA, 1981. Offset.

Myers, David. "Nicaragua." *Mesoamerica* 4 (April 1985), p. 7.

National Institute Ausberto Gutiérrez Ponce. "Utilidad del Jengibre en Nicaragua." Project submitted to the Third National Science and Production Fair. Managua: Department of Secondary Education/MED, 1983. Mimeographed.

National Network in Solidarity with the Nicaraguan People. "Atlantic Coast: Miskitu Crisis and Counterrevolution." In *The Nicaraguan Reader,* edited by Peter Rosset and John Vandermeer, pp. 83–90. New York: Grove Press, 1983.

_____. "Pueblo en Marcha: Adult Education in Nicaragua." In *The Nicaragua Reader,* edited by Peter Rosset and John Vandermeer, pp. 337–40. New York: Grove Press, 1983.

"Nicaragua." In *Encyclopedia of the Third World,* Second Volume, edited by George Thomas Kurian, pp. 1299–1314. New York: Facts on File, 1978.

Nolan, David. *FSLN: The Ideology of the Sandinistas and the Nicaraguan Revolution.* Coral Gables: Institute of Interamerican Studies, University of Miami, 1984.

Parsons, Talcott. "The School as a Social System." *Harvard Educational Review* 29 (1959): 297–318.

Paulston, Rolland. "Social and Educational Change: Conceptual Framework," *Comparative Education Review* 21 (June/October 1977): 370–94.

_____ and Henderson Franklin, Fay. "U.S. Professors in Nicaraguan Universities: The LASPAU/AID Managua Project." Cambridge: LASPAU; and Managua: MED, November 1983. Mimeographed.

Petras, James. "Whither the Nicaraguan Revolution?" *Monthly Review* 31 (October 1979): 1–22.

"Pluralism and Popular Power: An Interview with Sergio Ramírez Mercado." *Contemporary Marxism* 8 (Spring 1984): 169–73.

Ramírez, William. "El Problema Indígena y la Amenaza Imperialista en Nicaragua." *Barricada, Vergara,* January 6, 1982, pp. 13–14.

"Retroguardia de Jovenes Dispuestos a Combatir." *Barricada,* May 26, 1984, p. 8.

Rius (Eduardo del Río). *Nicaragua for Beginners.* New York: Writers and Readers Publishing, Inc., 1984.

Rosales Herrera, Guillermo. "Análisis de la Estructura y Funcionamiento de la Administración del Sistema Educativo Nicaragüense a Nivel Oficial." In *Educación y Dependencia,* edited by Instituto de Promoción Humana. Managua: Institute for Human Promotion, INPRHU, 1976.

Rosen, Stanley. "Recentralization, Decentralization and Rationalization: Deng Xiaoping's Bifurcated Educational Policy." *Modern China* 10 (July 1985).

Rosset, Peter and John Vandermeer, eds. *The Nicaragua Reader.* New York: Grove Press, 1983.

Rothschuh,Tablada, Guillermo and Carlos Tamez, La Cruzada Nacional de Alfabetización de Nicaragua: Su Organización y Estrategias de Participación y Mobilización. Paris: UNESCO, 1983.

Sandinista Youth Association. *Sabes lo Que Pasa en la JS 19 de Julio.* Managua: JS–19 J, 1981. Offset.

Sobel, Irvin. "The Human Capital Revolution in Economic Development," *Comparative Education Review* 22 (June 1978): 267–308.

Stansifer, Charles L. "The Nicaraguan National Literacy Crusade," American University Field Staff Reports, South America, No. 41, 1981.

Thome, Joseph R., and David Kaimowitz. "Agrarian Reform." In *Nicaragua: The First Five Years,* edited by Thomas W. Walker, pp. 299–315. New York: Praeger, 1985.

Torres, Rosa María. *De Alfabetizando a Maestro Popular: La Post-Alfabetización en Nicaragua.* Managua: Institute of Economic and Social Research, INIES, 1983.

Treumann, Beverly. "Nicaragua's Second Revolution." *Christianity and Crisis* 41 (November 2, 1981): 291–302.

Tünnermann Bernheim, Carlos. "Cincos Años de Educación en la Revolución." Managua: Ministry of Education, 1984. Mimeographed.

_____. *Hacia una Nueva Educación.* Managua: Ministry of Education, 1980.

_____. "One Year Later." In *Nicaragua for the Eradication of Illiteracy,* edited by Jan Kaspar. Paris: International Union of Students and UNESCO, n.d.

Tünnermann Bernheim, Carlos, interview. "Educating the People." In *Nicaragua—A New Kind of Revolution,* edited by Philip Zwerling and Connie Martin, pp. 64–81. Westport, Conn.: Lawrence Hill, 1985.

United Nations Economic Commission for Latin America. "Nicaragua: Repercusiones Económicas de los Acontecimientos Políticos Recientes." Mexico City: UN/ECLA, August 1979.

United Nations Educational, Scientific and Cultural Organization. *Educational and Cultural Development Project: Nicaragua.* Paris: UNESCO, March 1983.

_____. *1983 Statistical Yearbook.* Paris: UNESCO, 1983.

Vargas Narváez, Mariano. "Situación Socio-Económica y Educación Superior Antes y Despues del Triunfo de la Revolución Popular Sandinista." Managua: National Higher Education Council, CNES, May 1983. Mimeographed.

Walker, Thomas W., ed. *Nicaragua: The First Five Years.* New York: Praeger, 1985.

_____. *Nicaragua: The Land of Sandino.* Boulder, Col.: Westview Press, 1981.

_____, ed. *Nicaragua in Revolution.* New York: Praeger, 1982.

Williamson, Bill. *Education, Social Structure and Development.* New York: Holmes & Meier, 1979.

Index

About the Author

Robert F. Arnove is Professor of Comparative and International Education at Indiana University, Bloomington. He has been a visiting professor at Stanford, McGill, and Hangzhou (PRC) Universities. His Praeger publications include *Student Alienation: A Venezuelan Study* (1971), and *Educational Television: A Policy Critique and Guide for Developing Countries* (1976). He is the editor of *Philanthropy and Cultural Imperialism: The Foundations at Home and Abroad,* and the co-editor of *Education and American Culture* and *Comparative Education.* He also is the producer of documentary films on alternative schools in the United States and the 1984 Nicaraguan elections. Professor Arnove has worked extensively in Latin America as an educational adviser and researcher. He received his doctorate from Stanford University in 1969 in the field of International Development Education.